Unicorn
Coloring Book

Adult Colouring Books

Aryla Publishing 2017

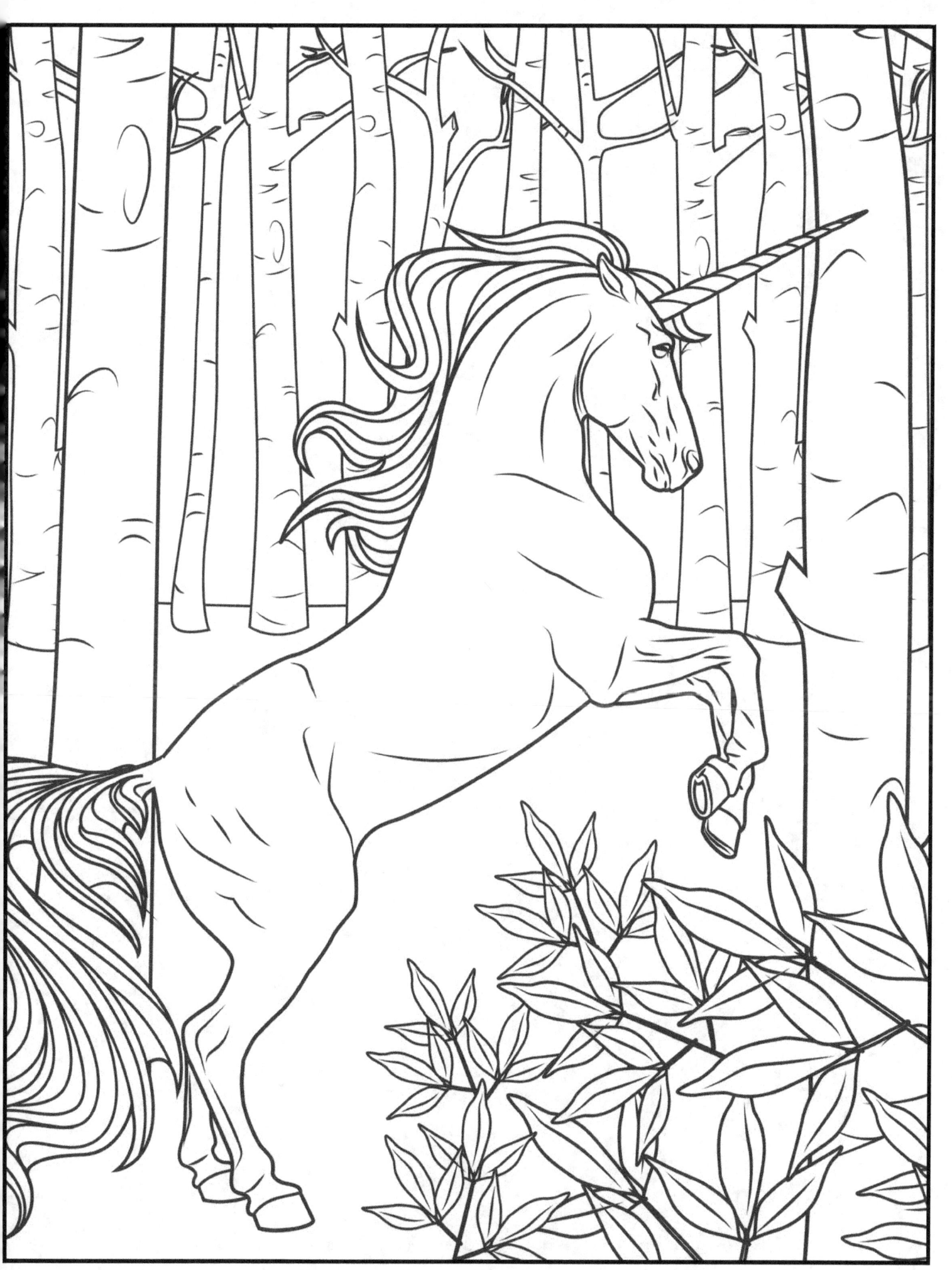

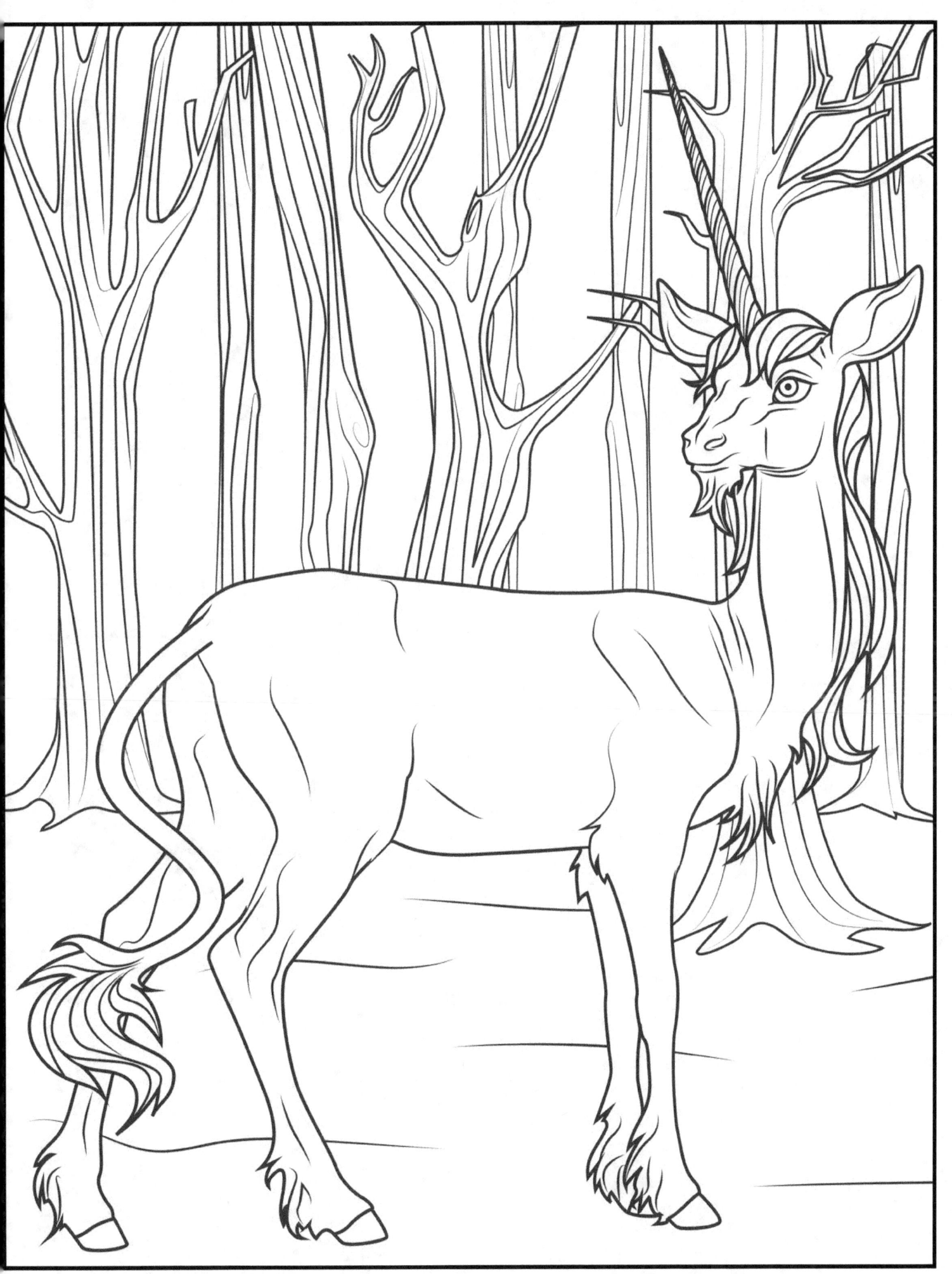

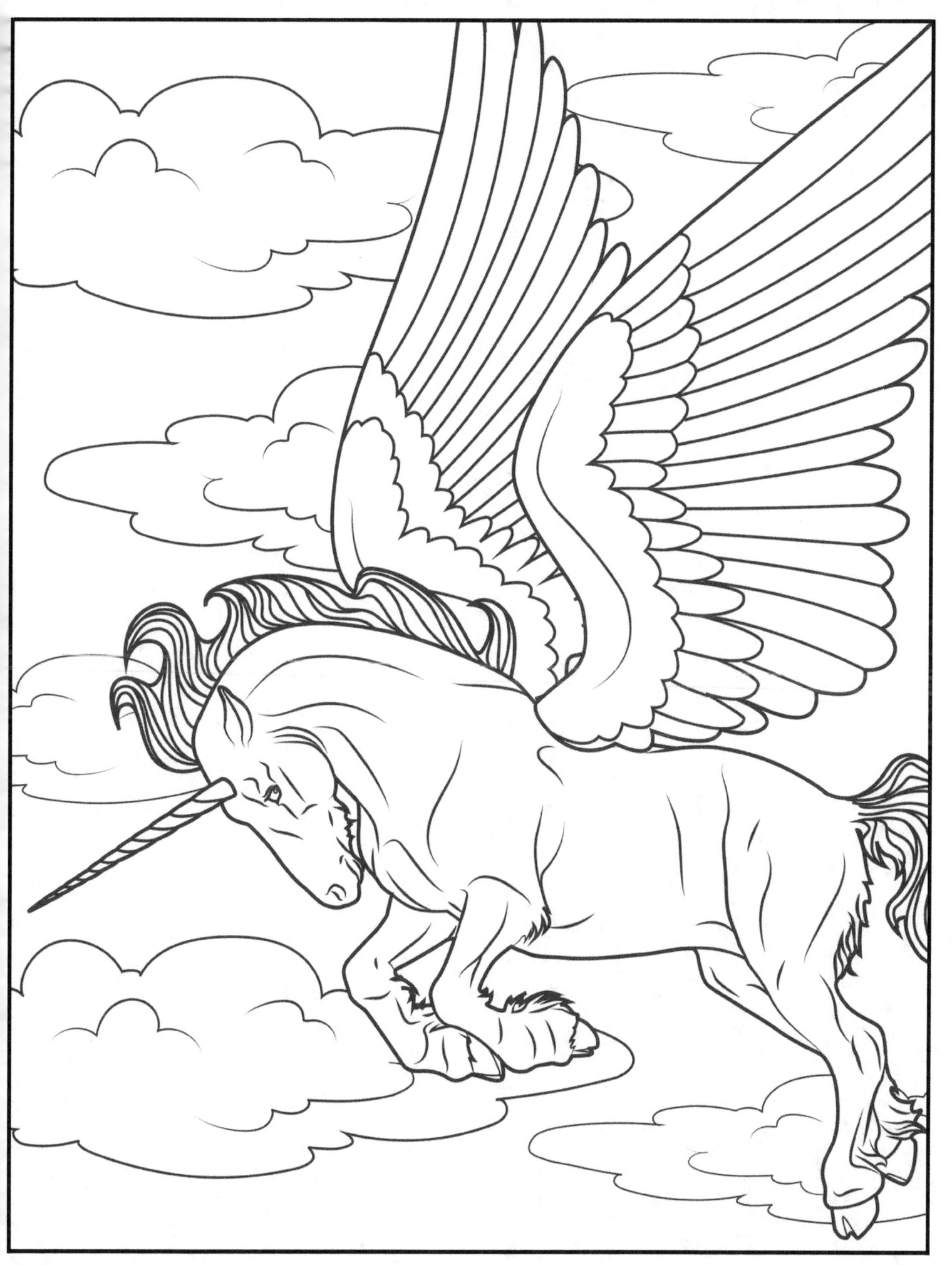

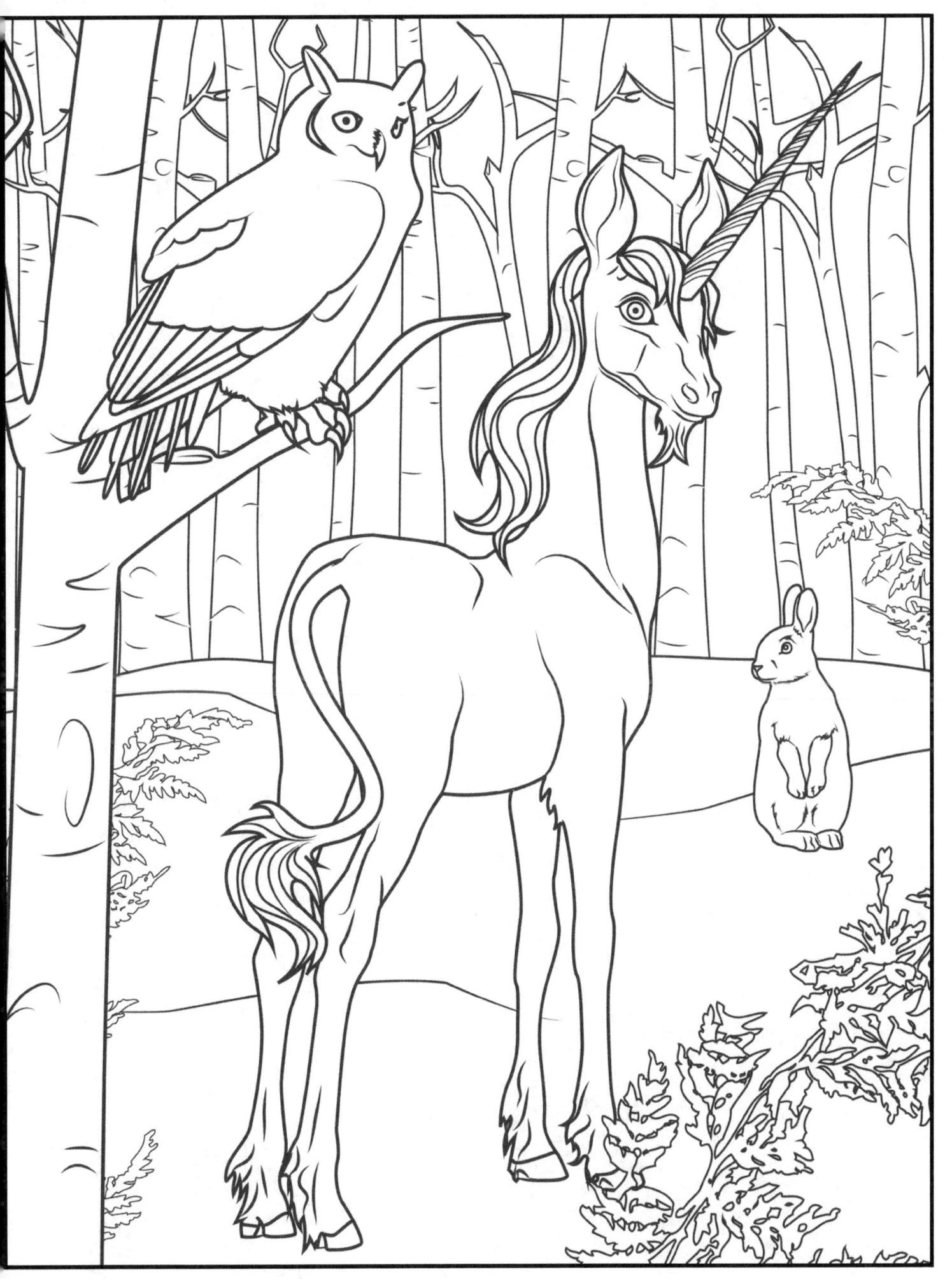

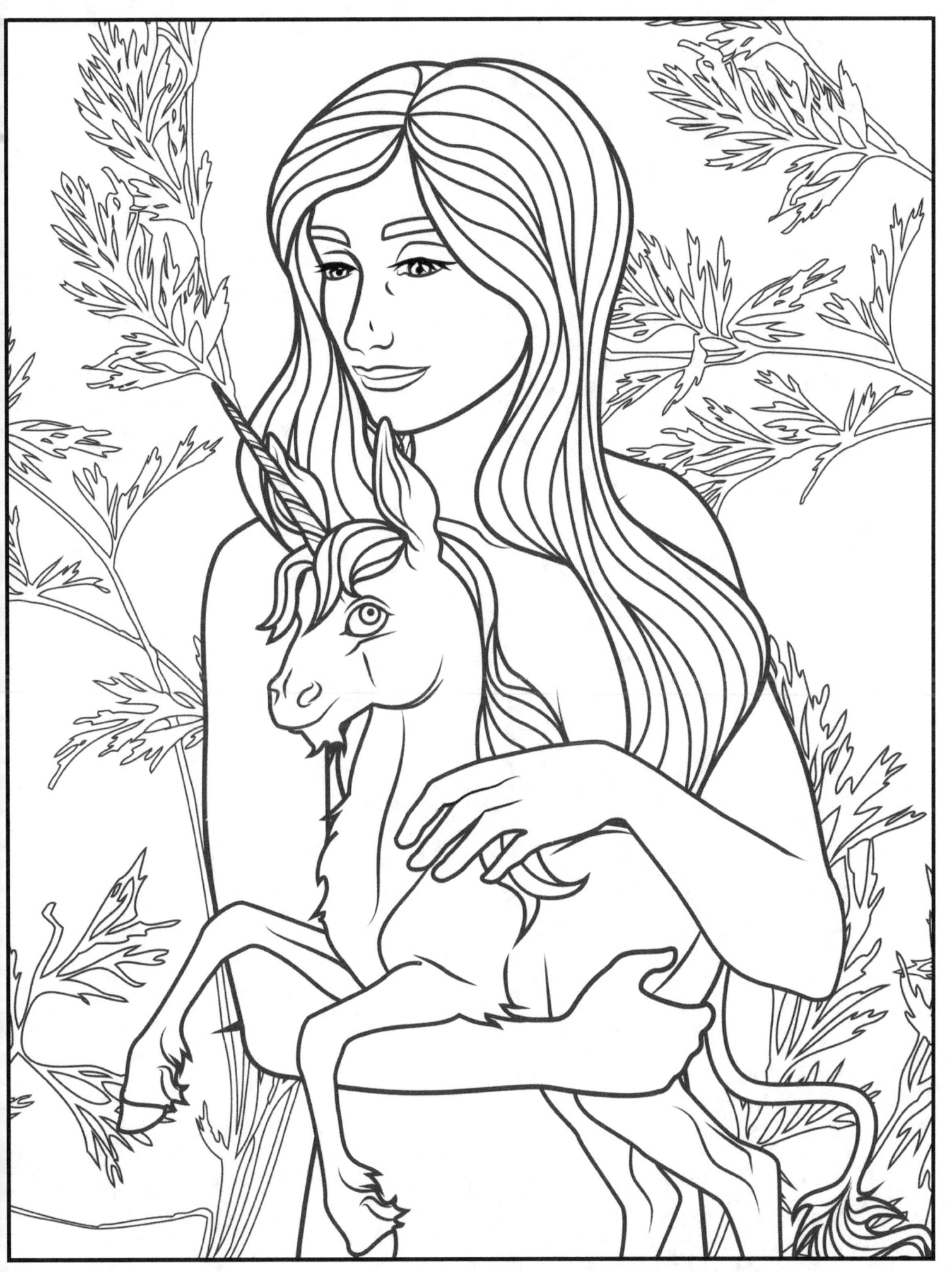

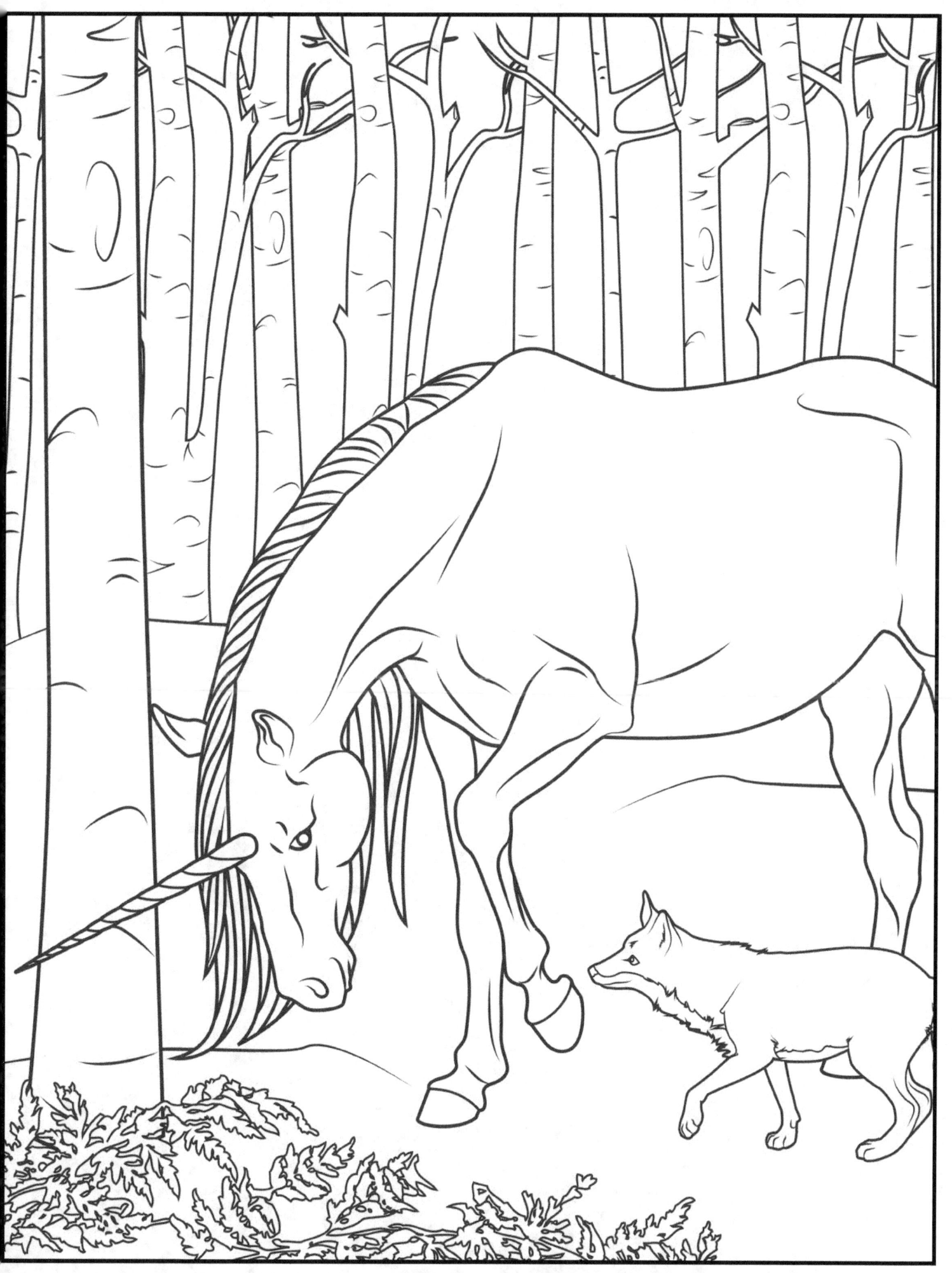

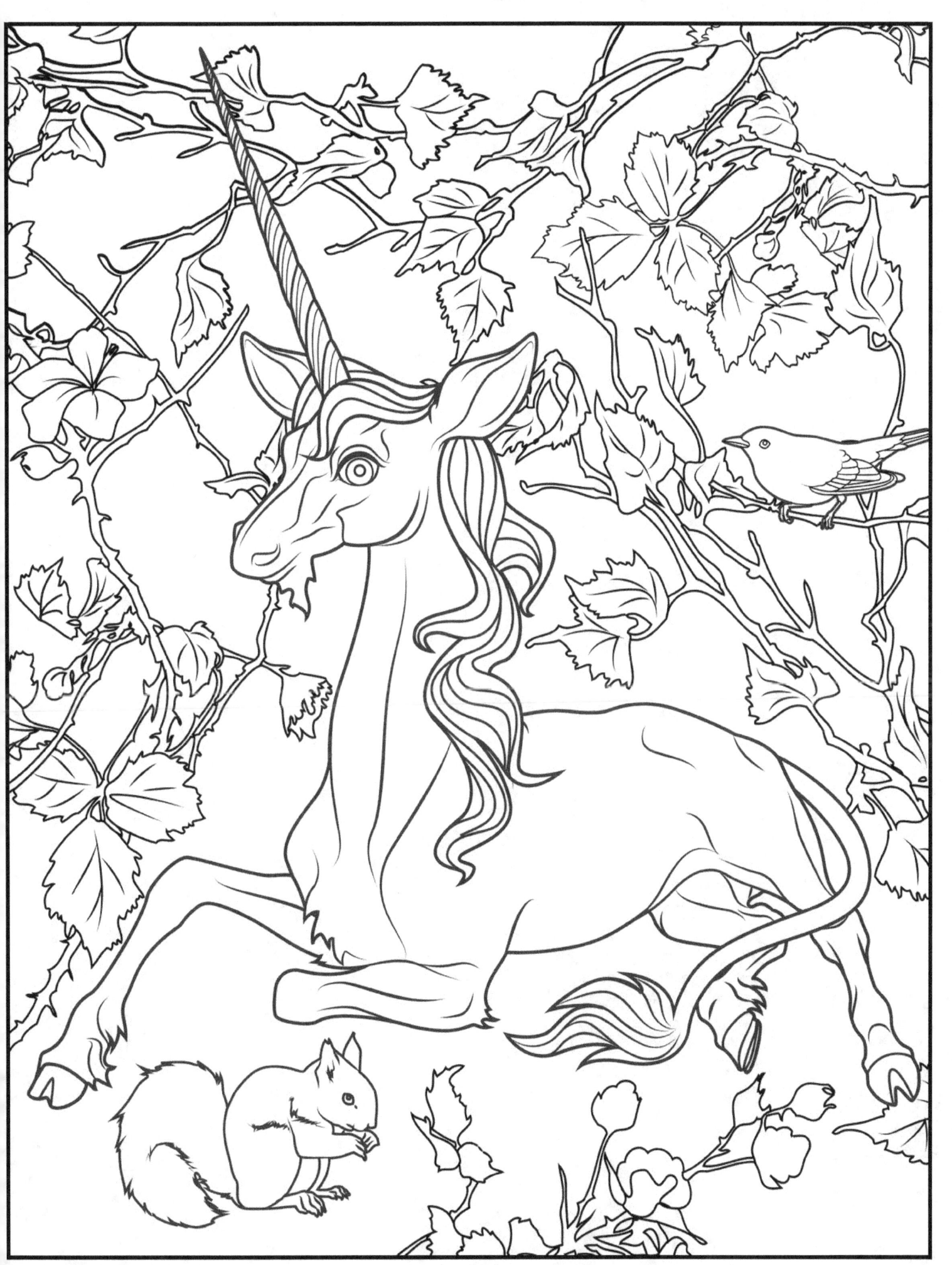

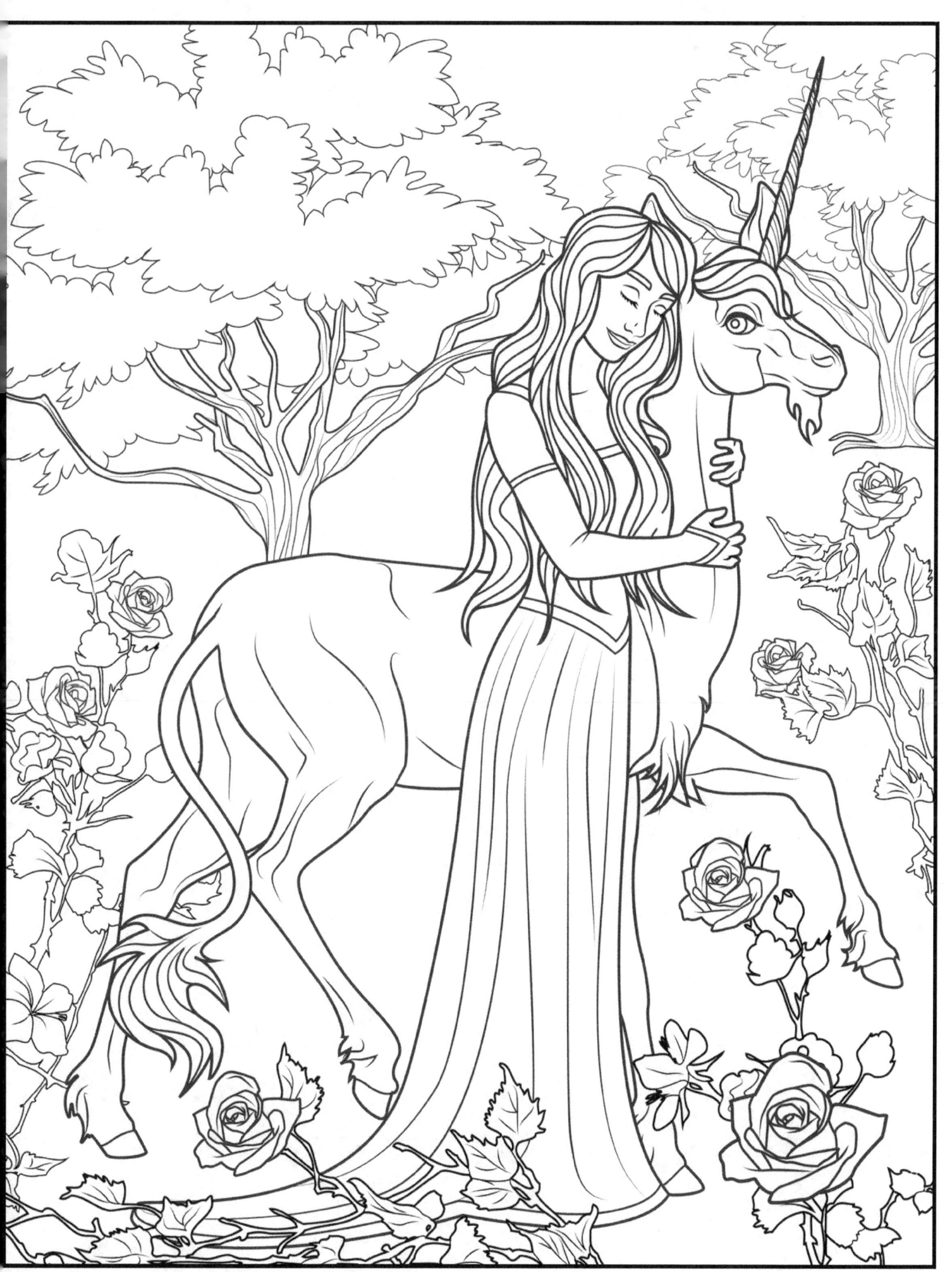

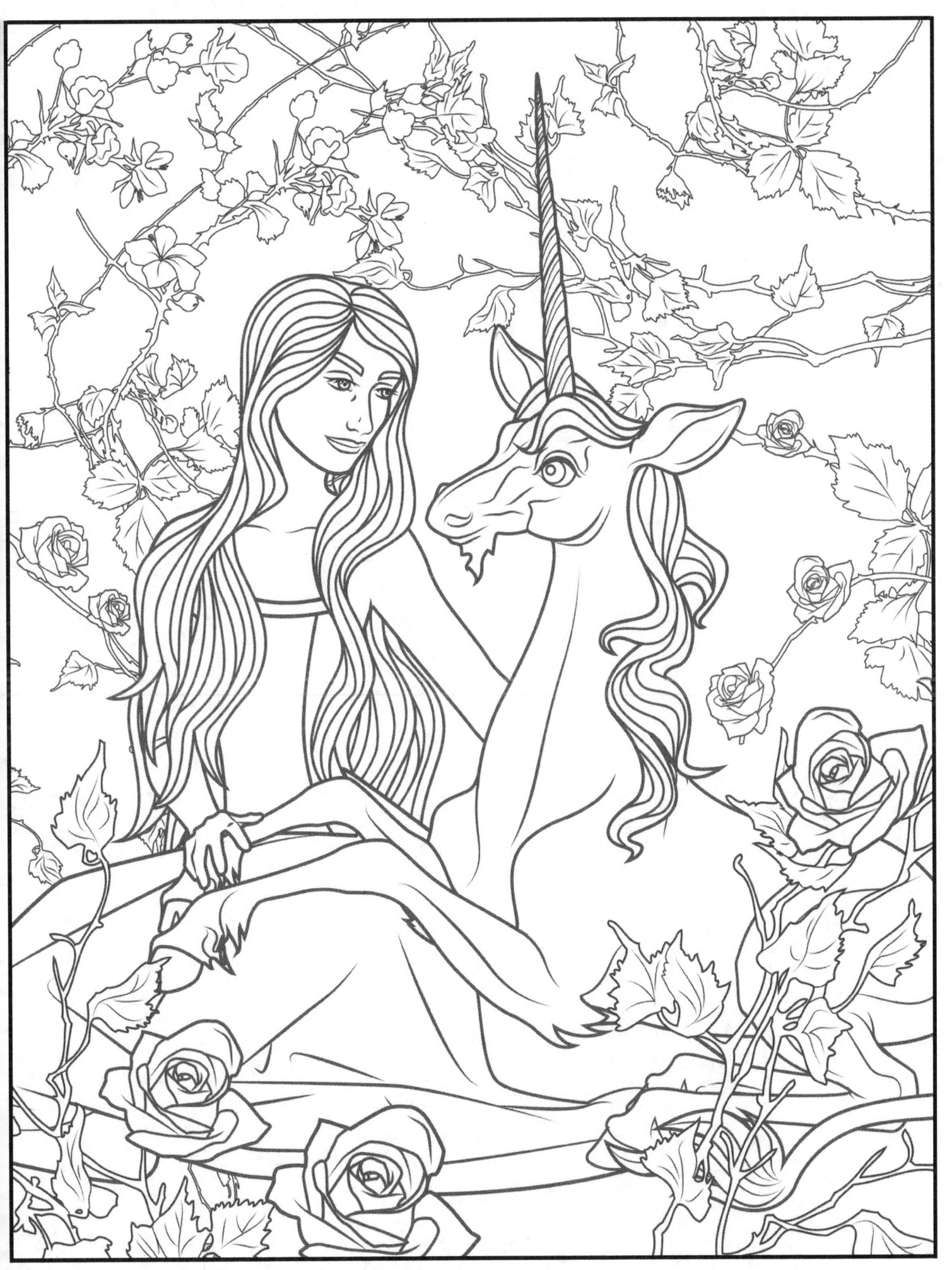

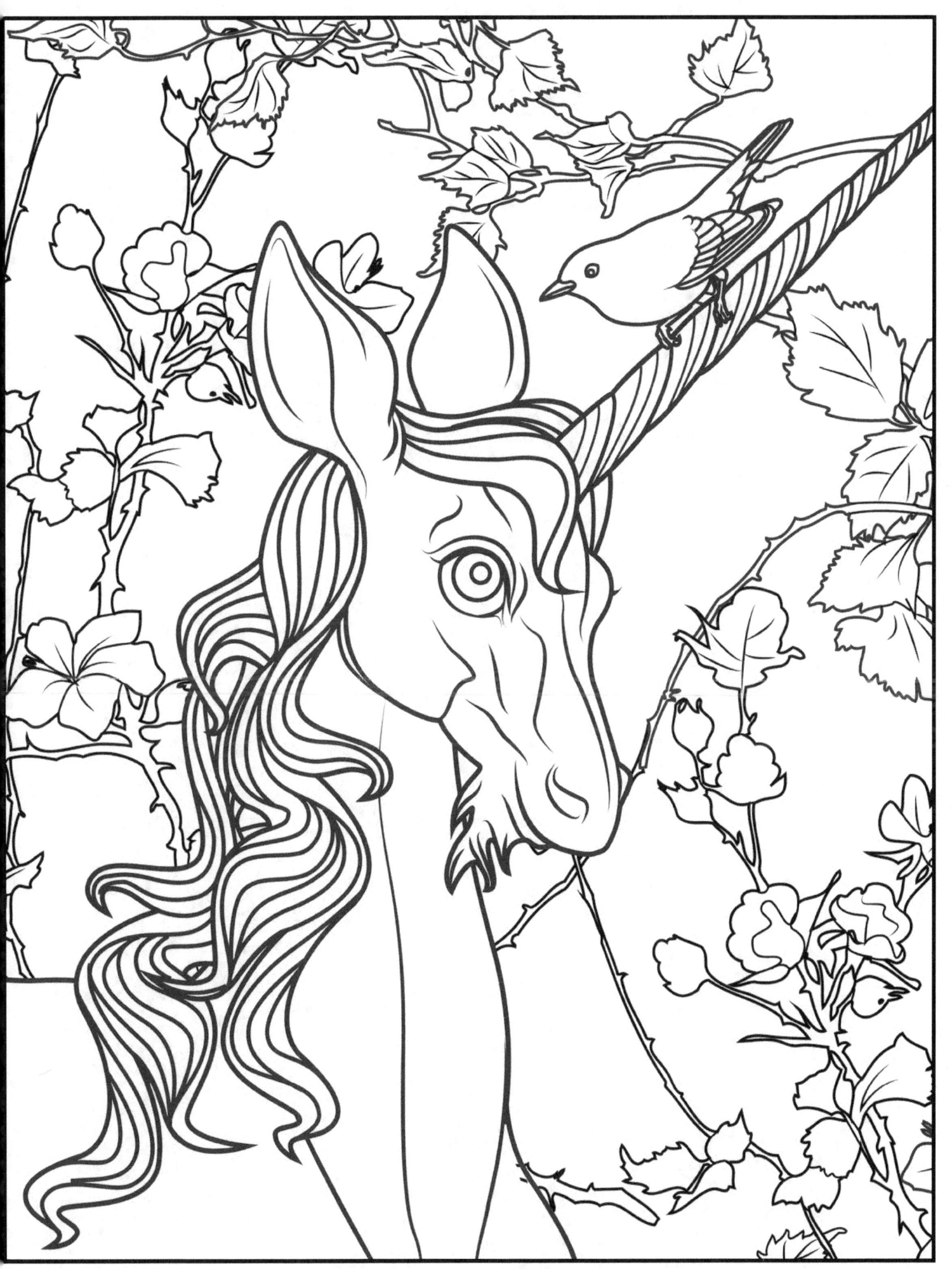

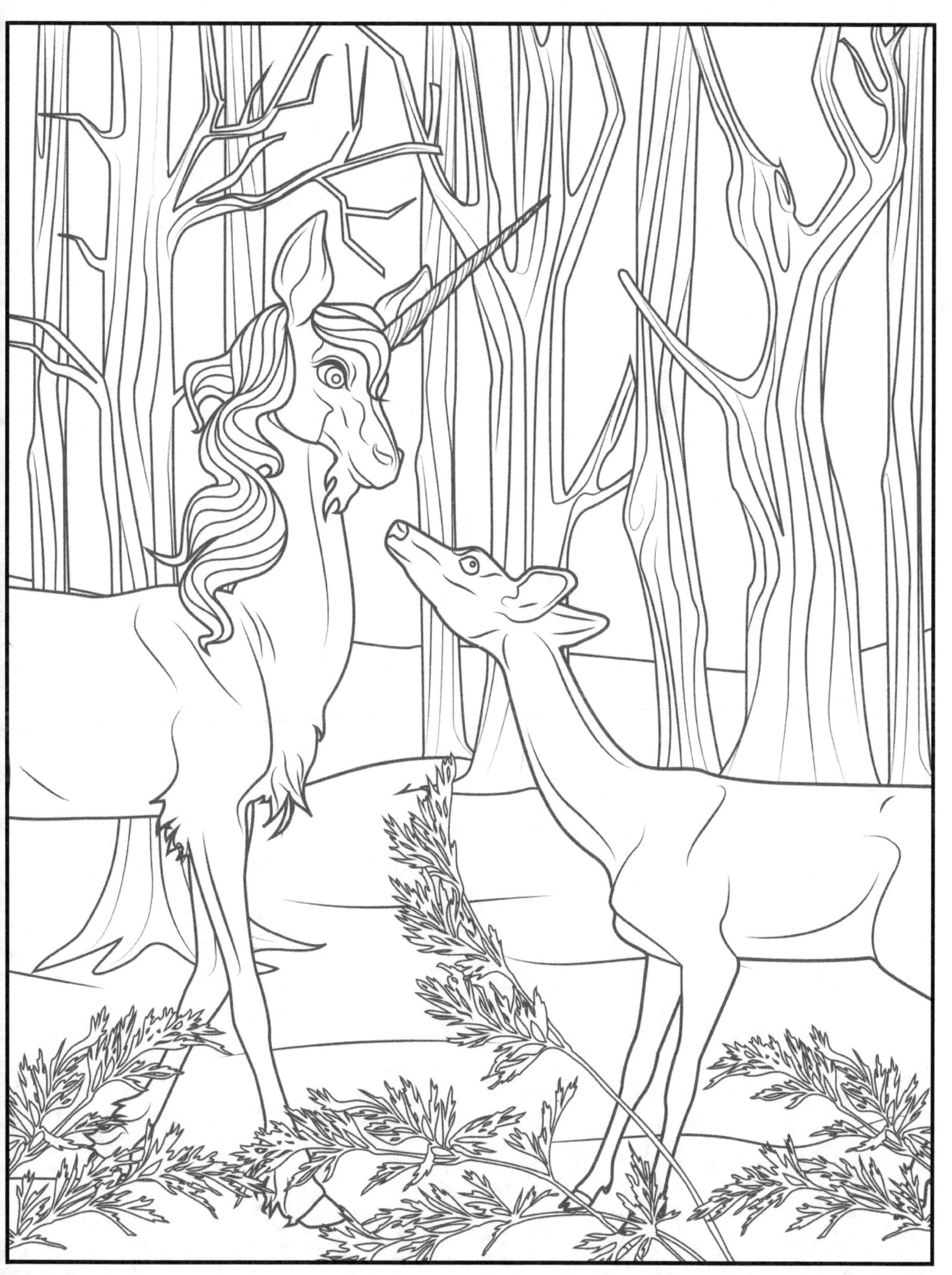

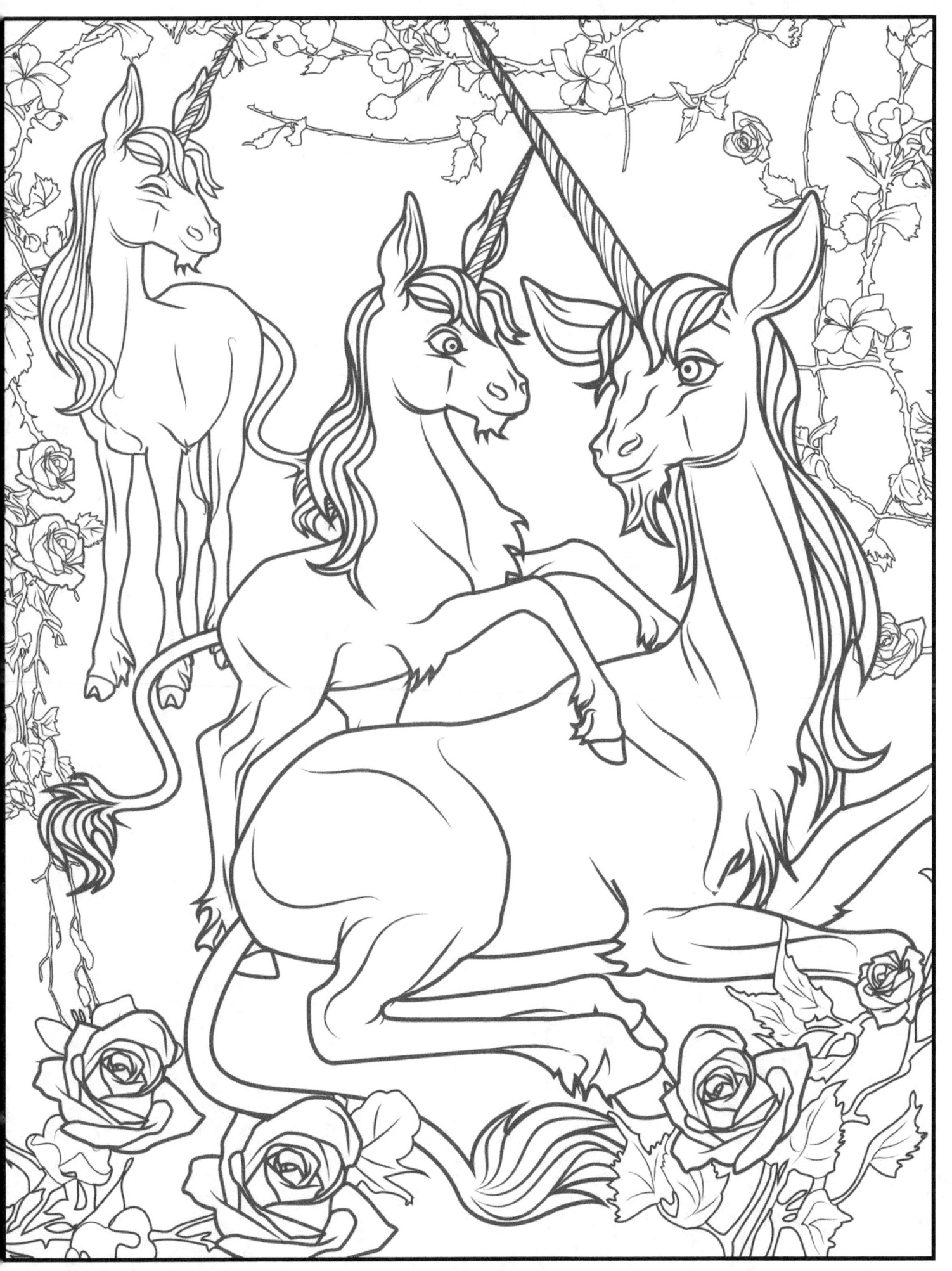

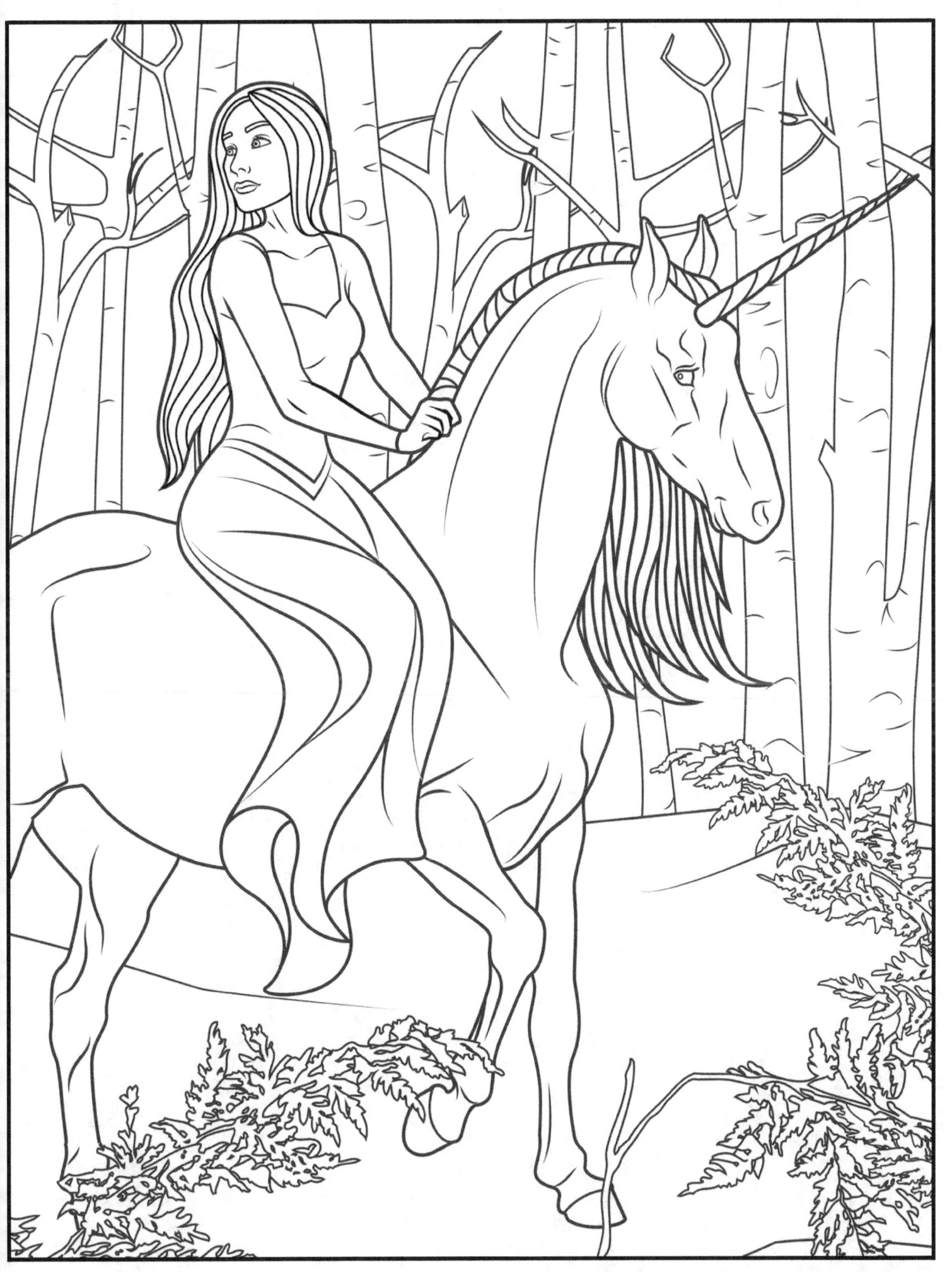

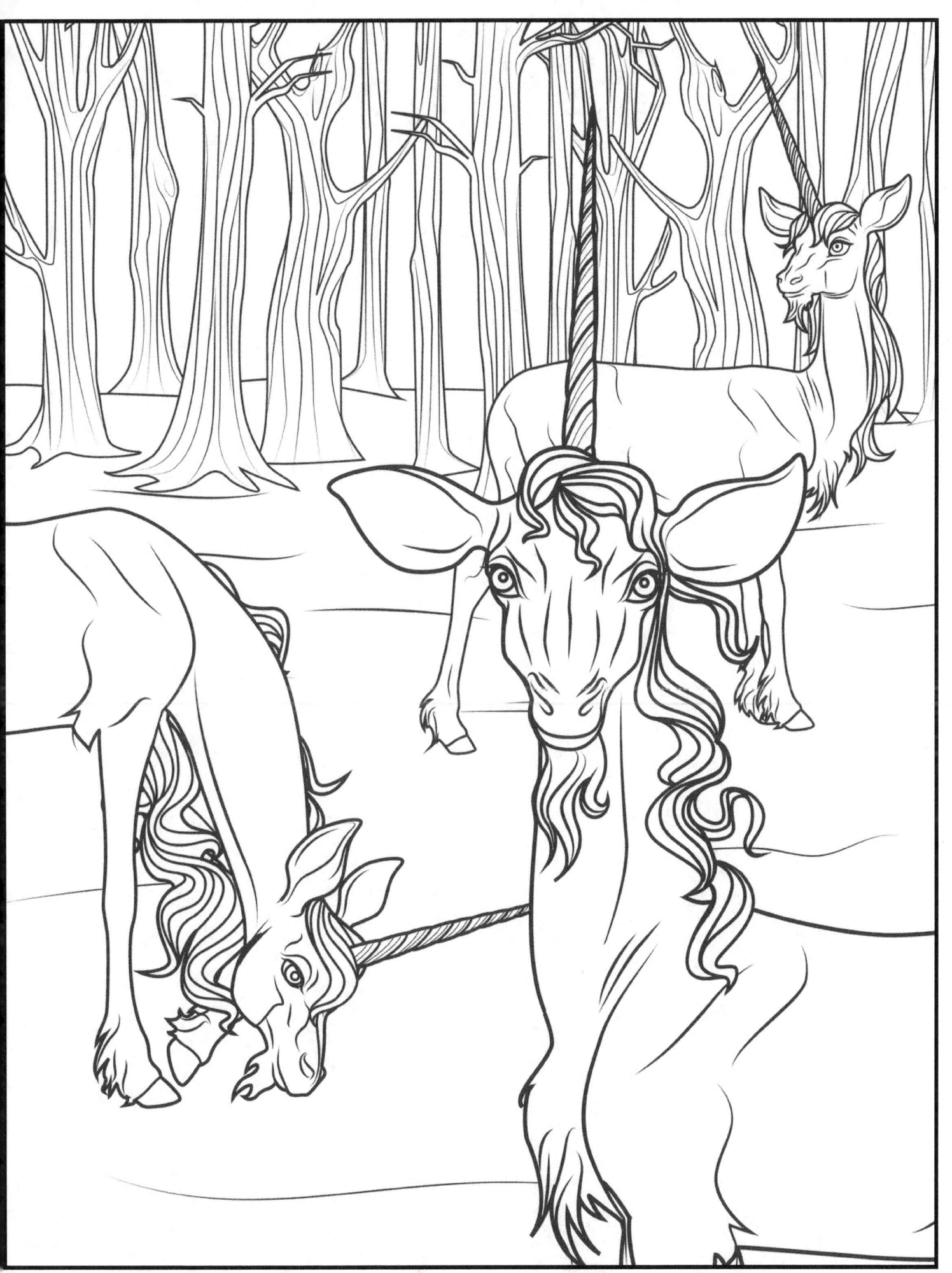

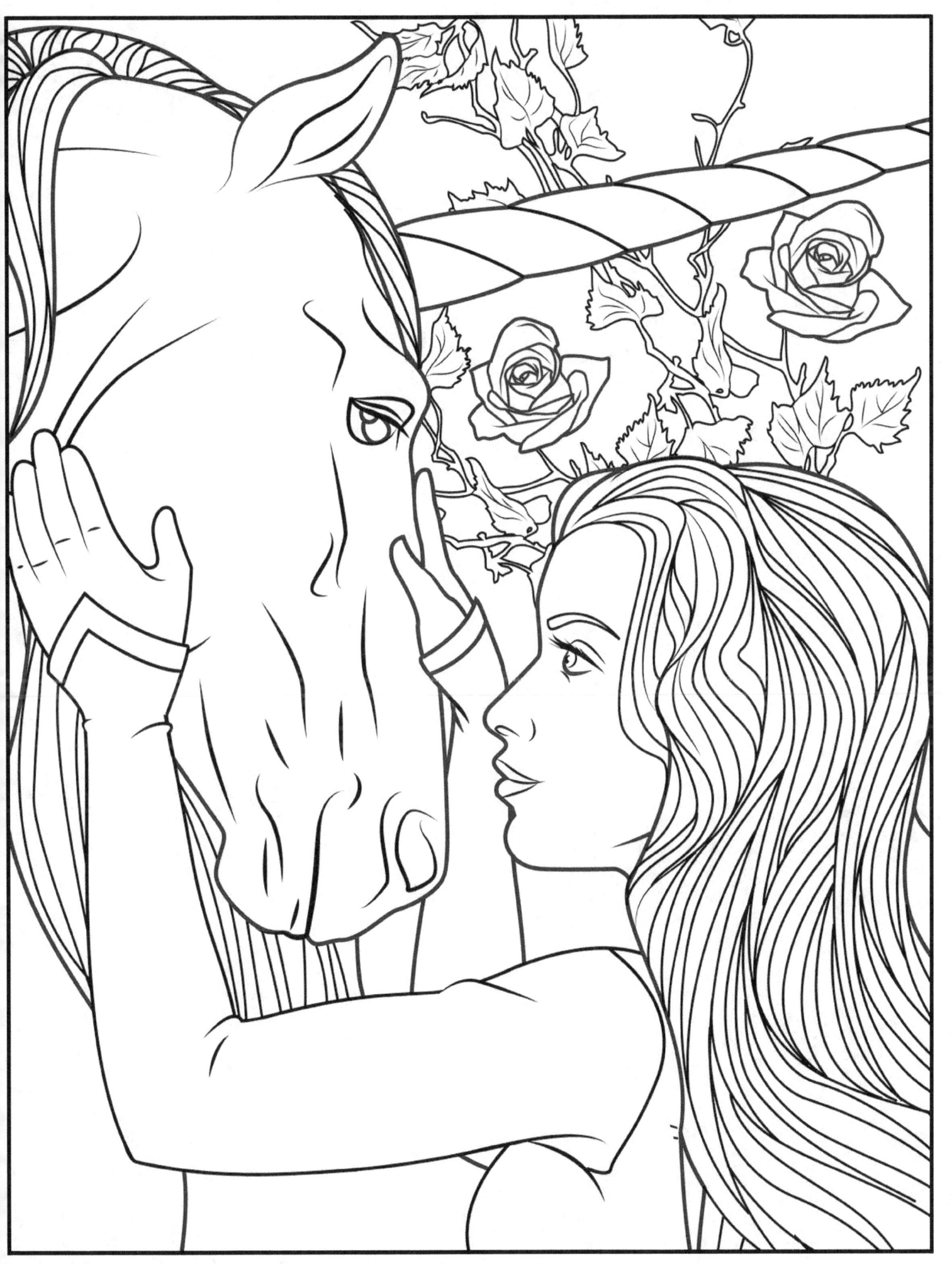

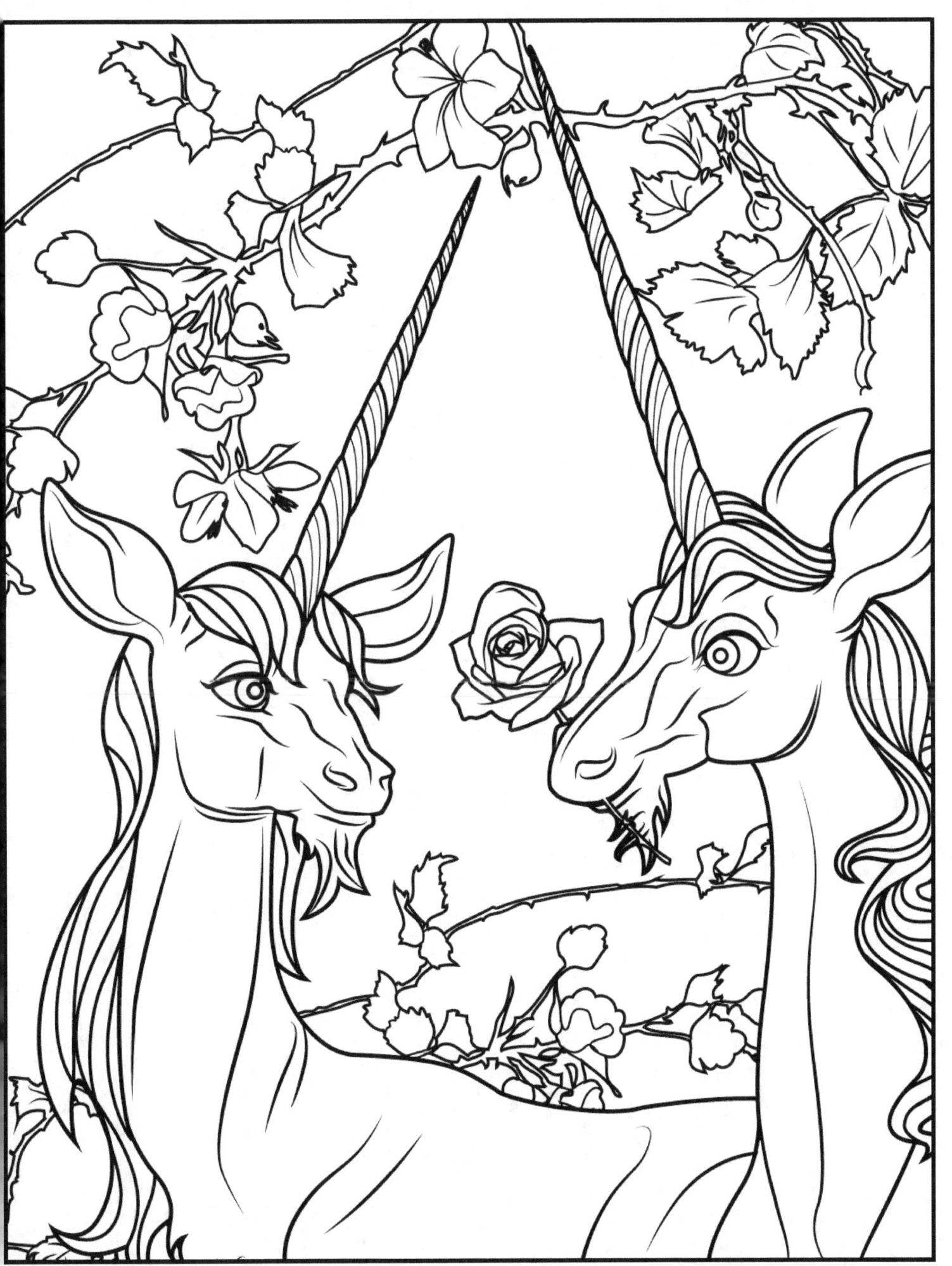

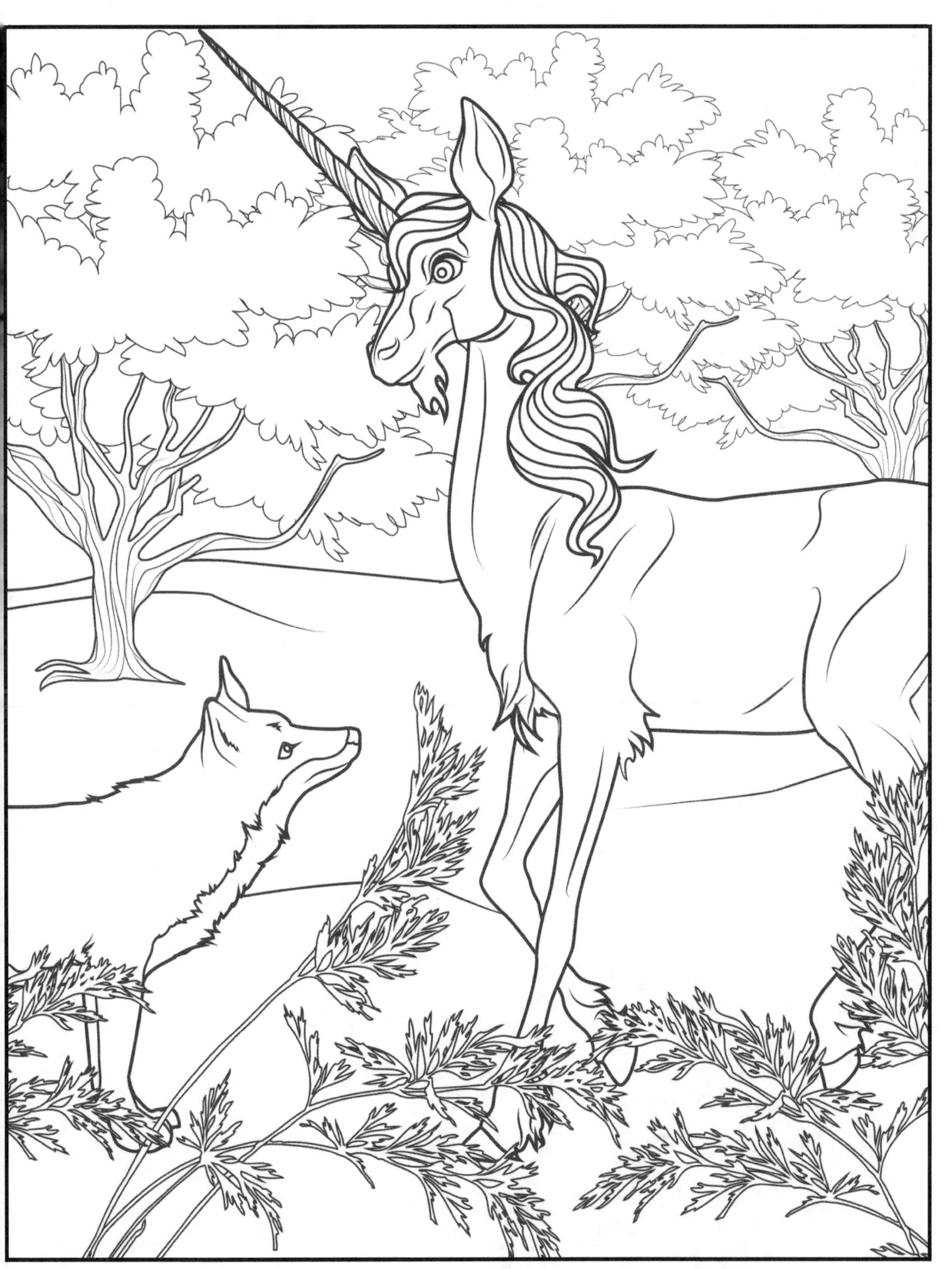

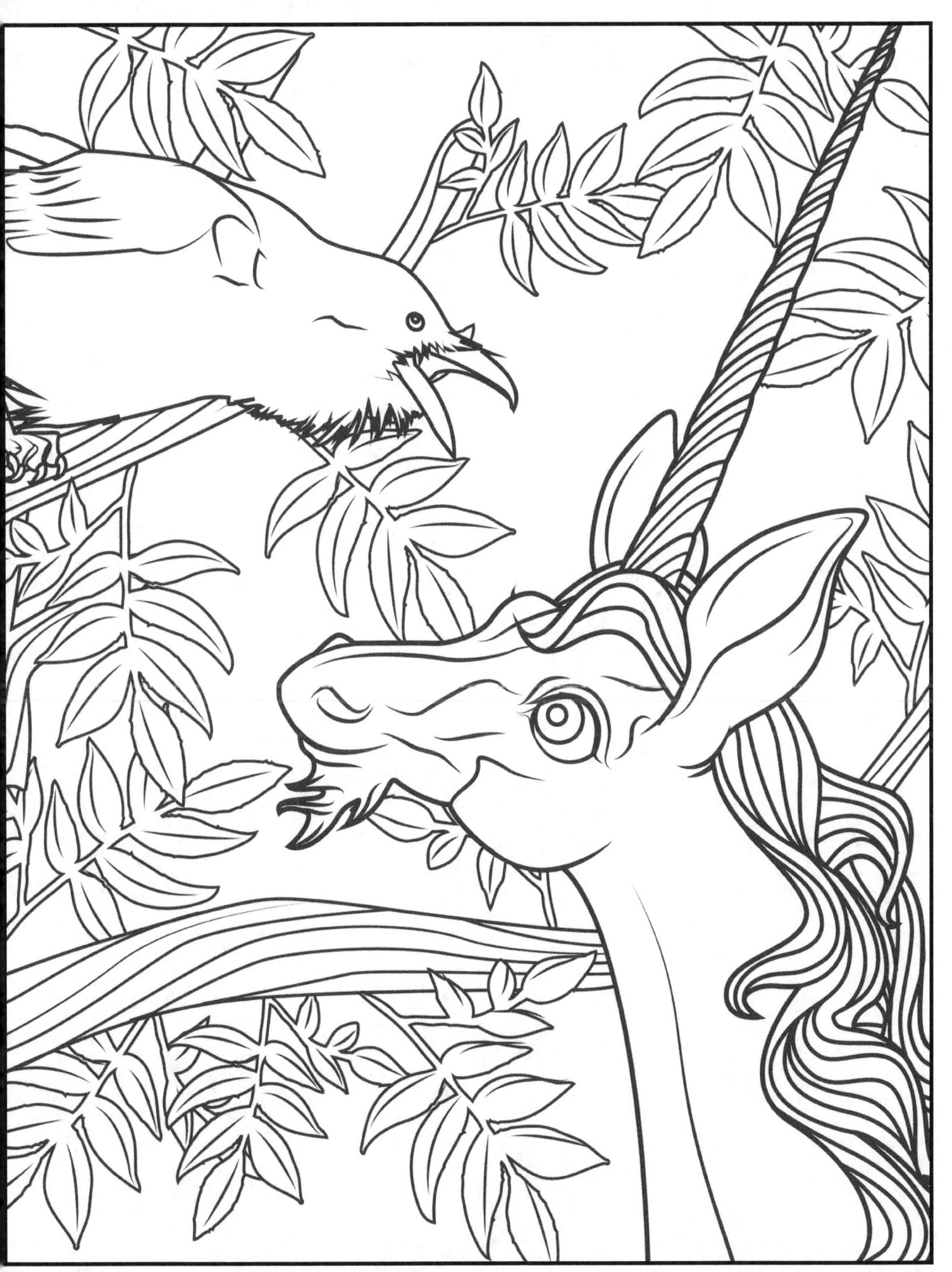

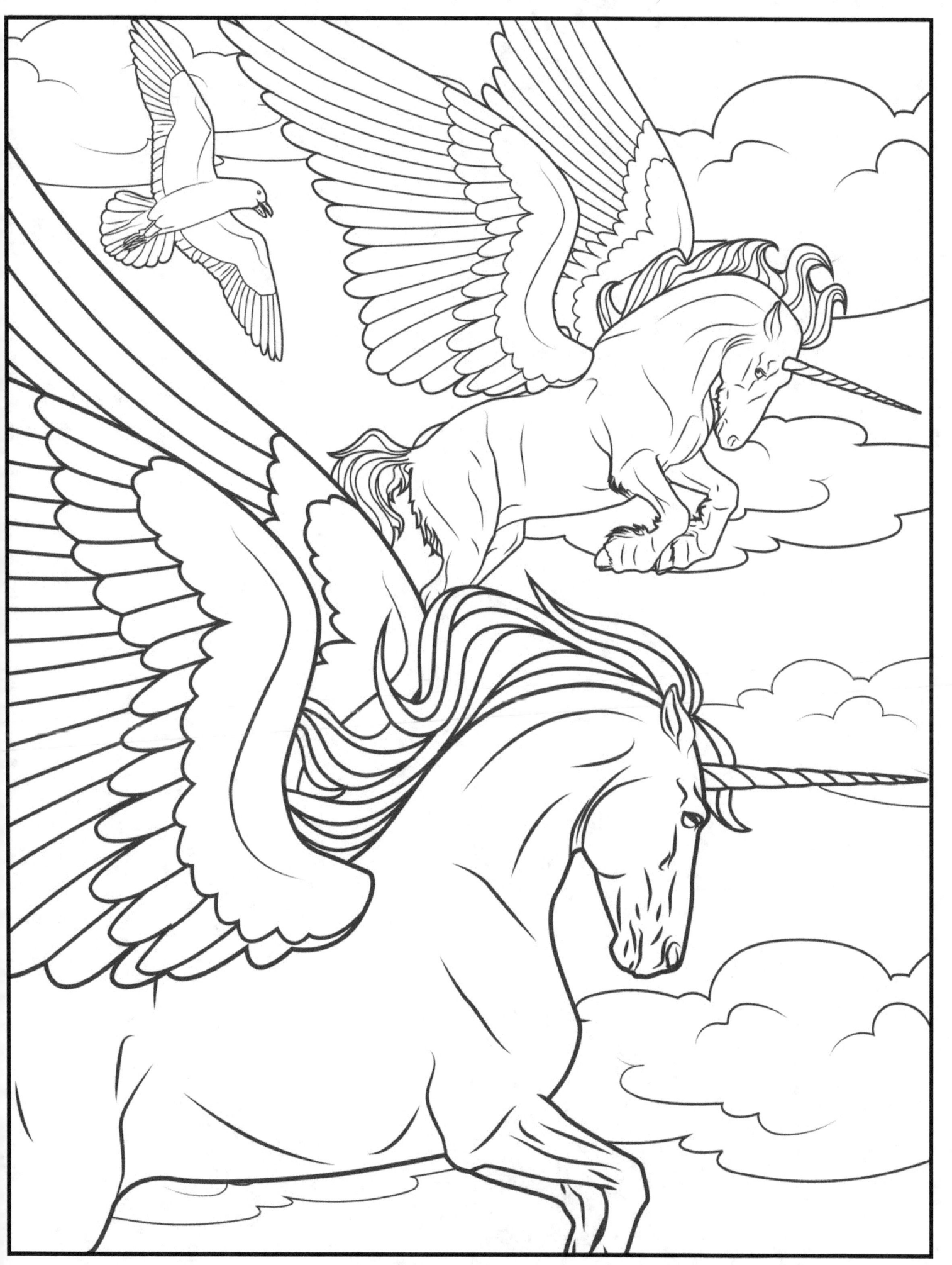

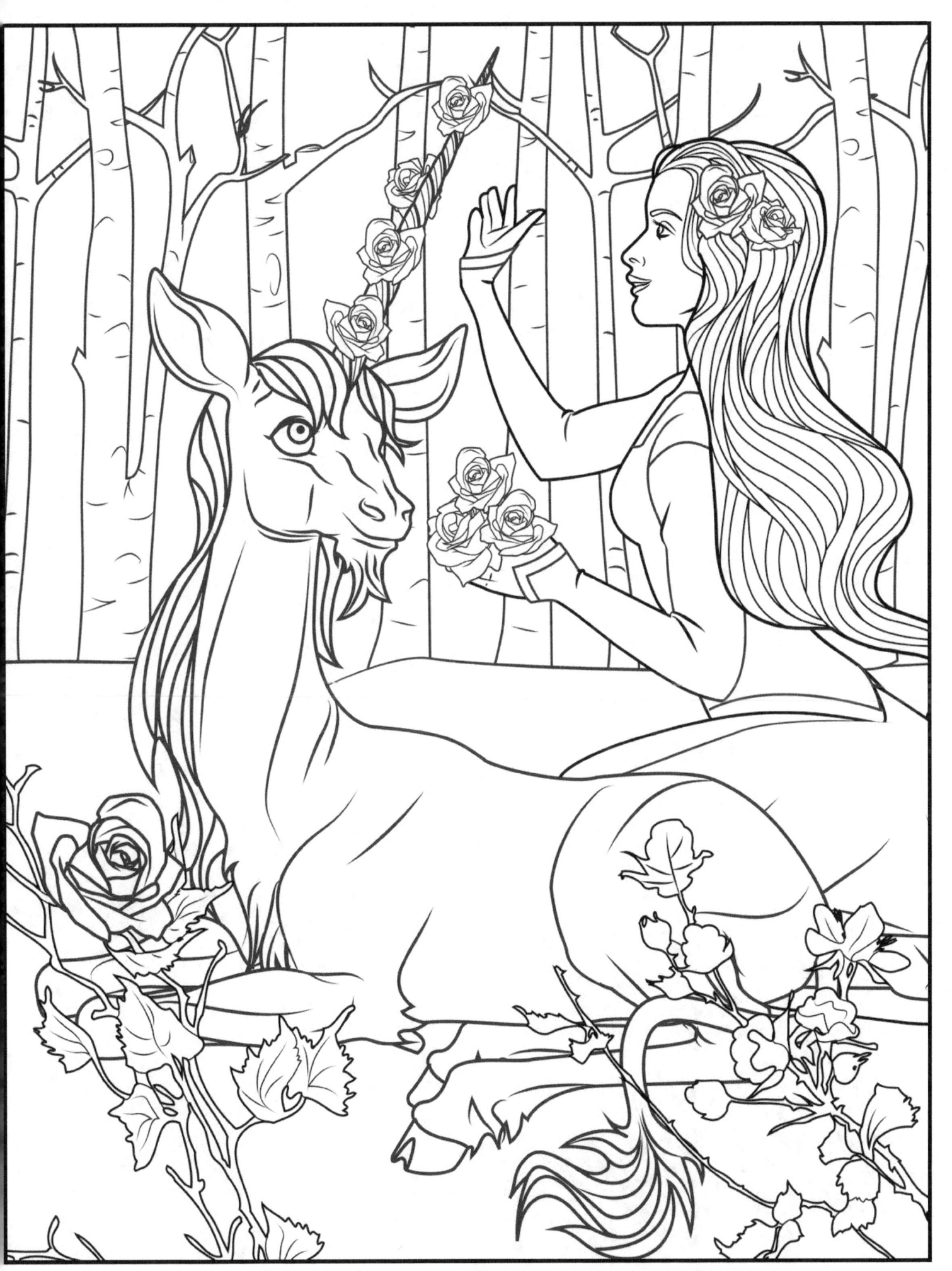

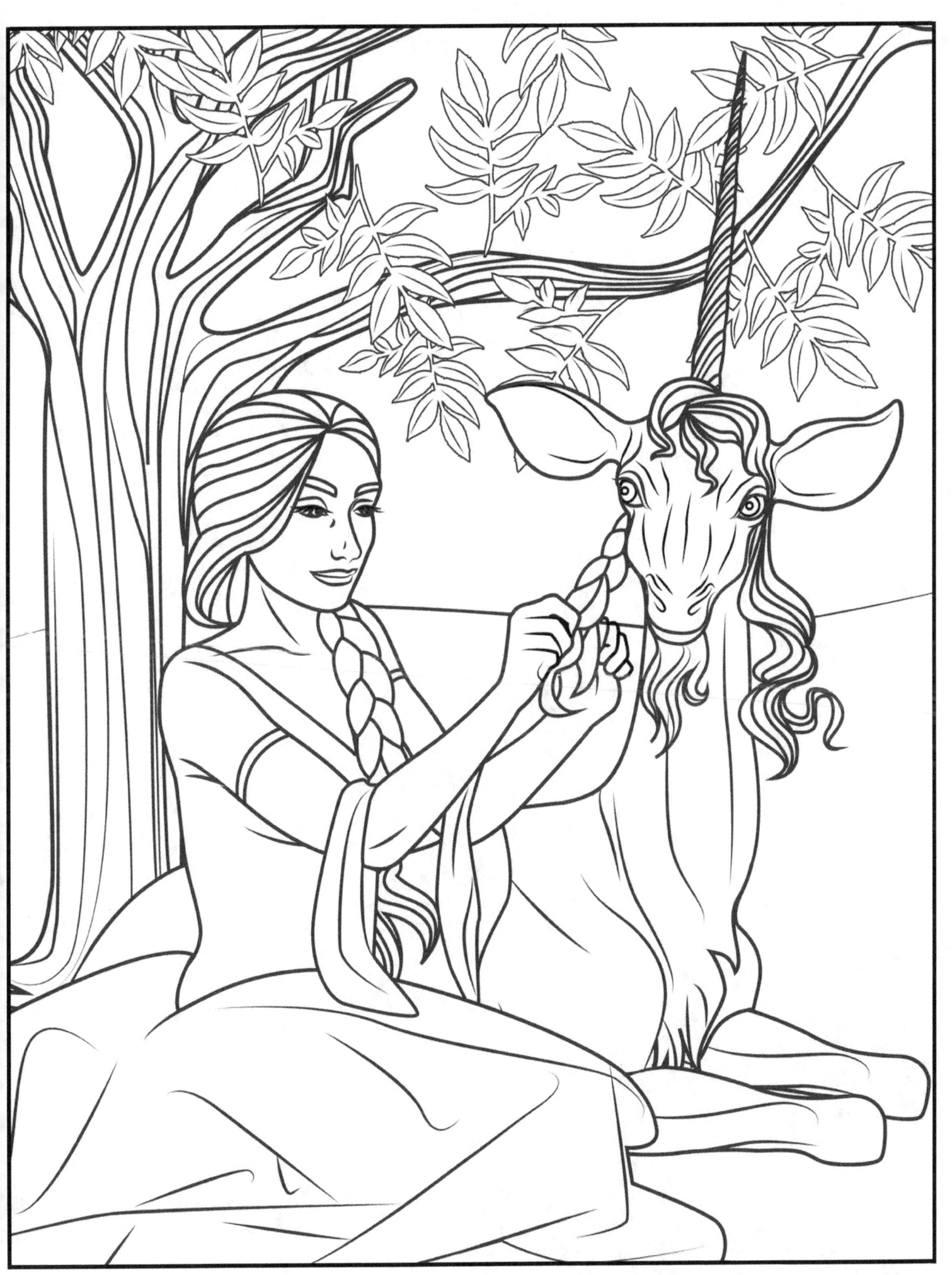

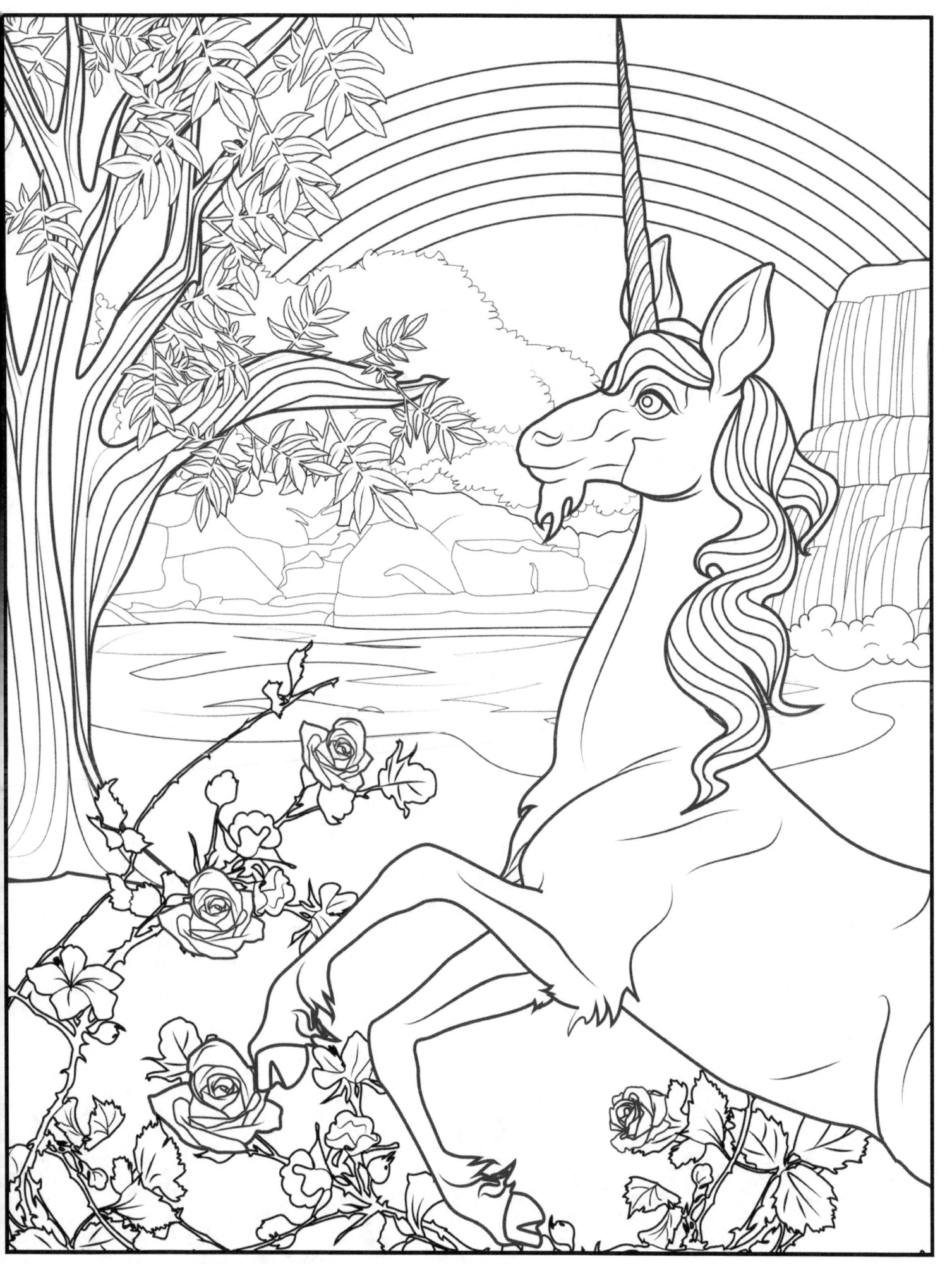

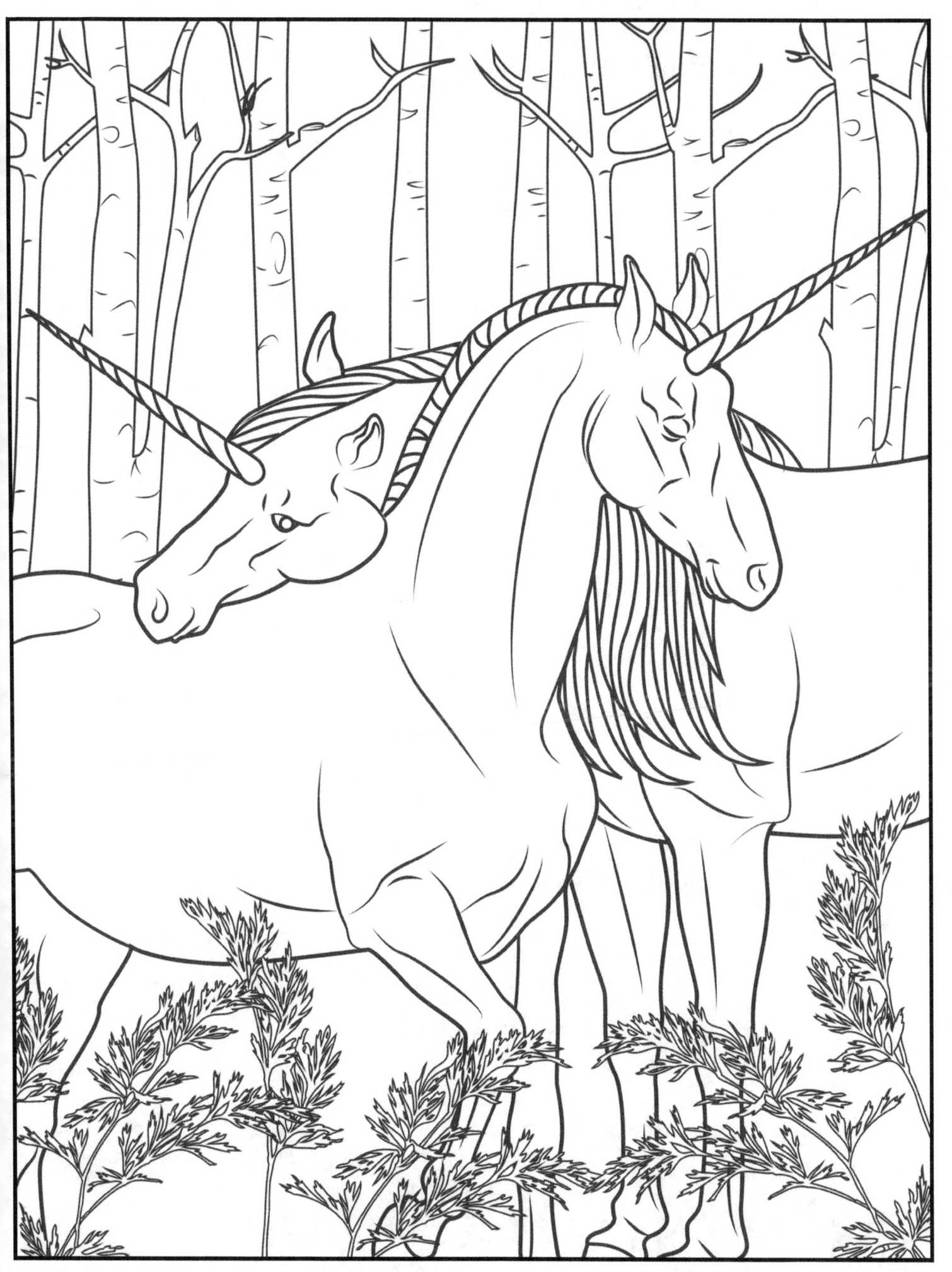

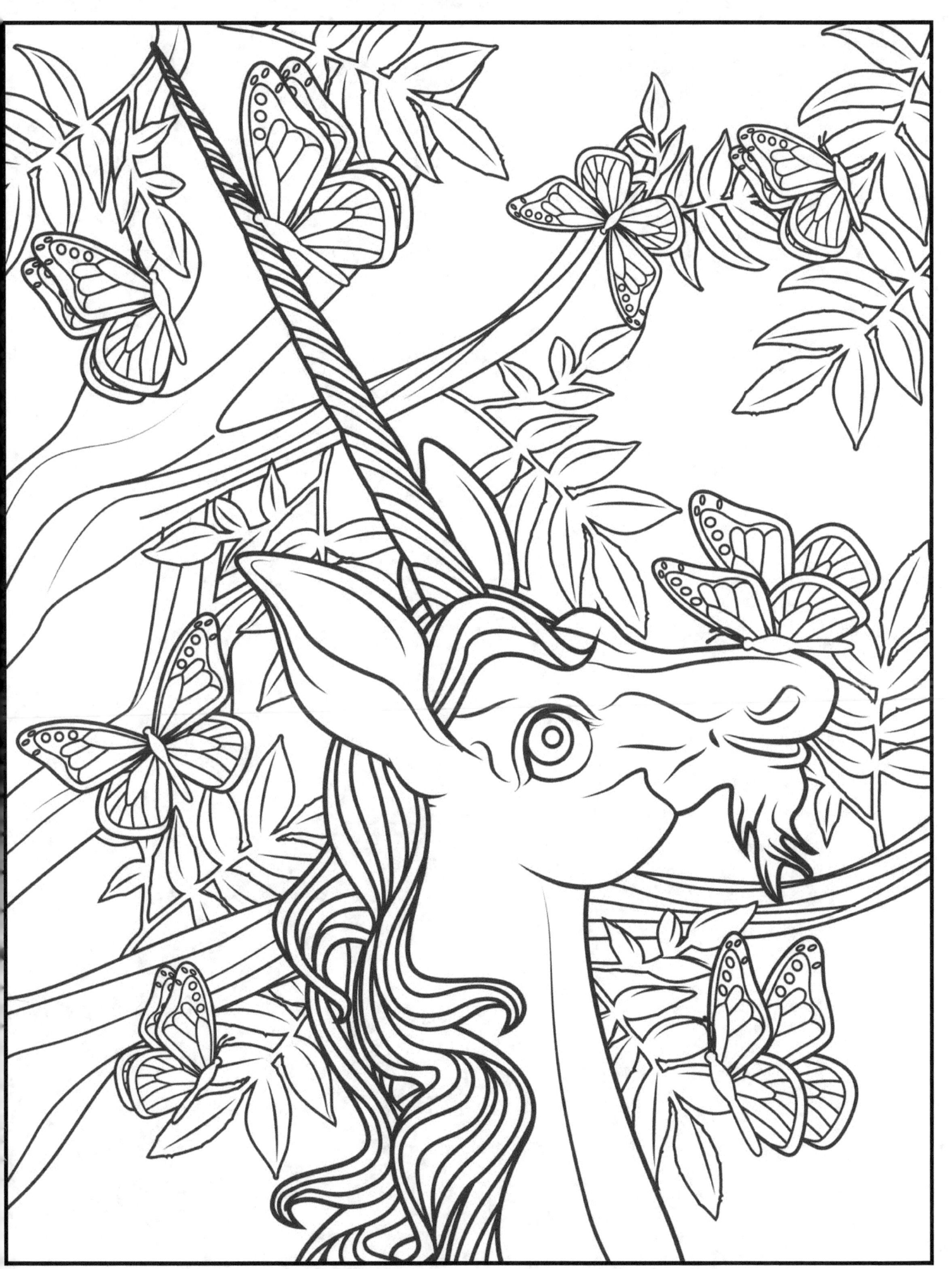

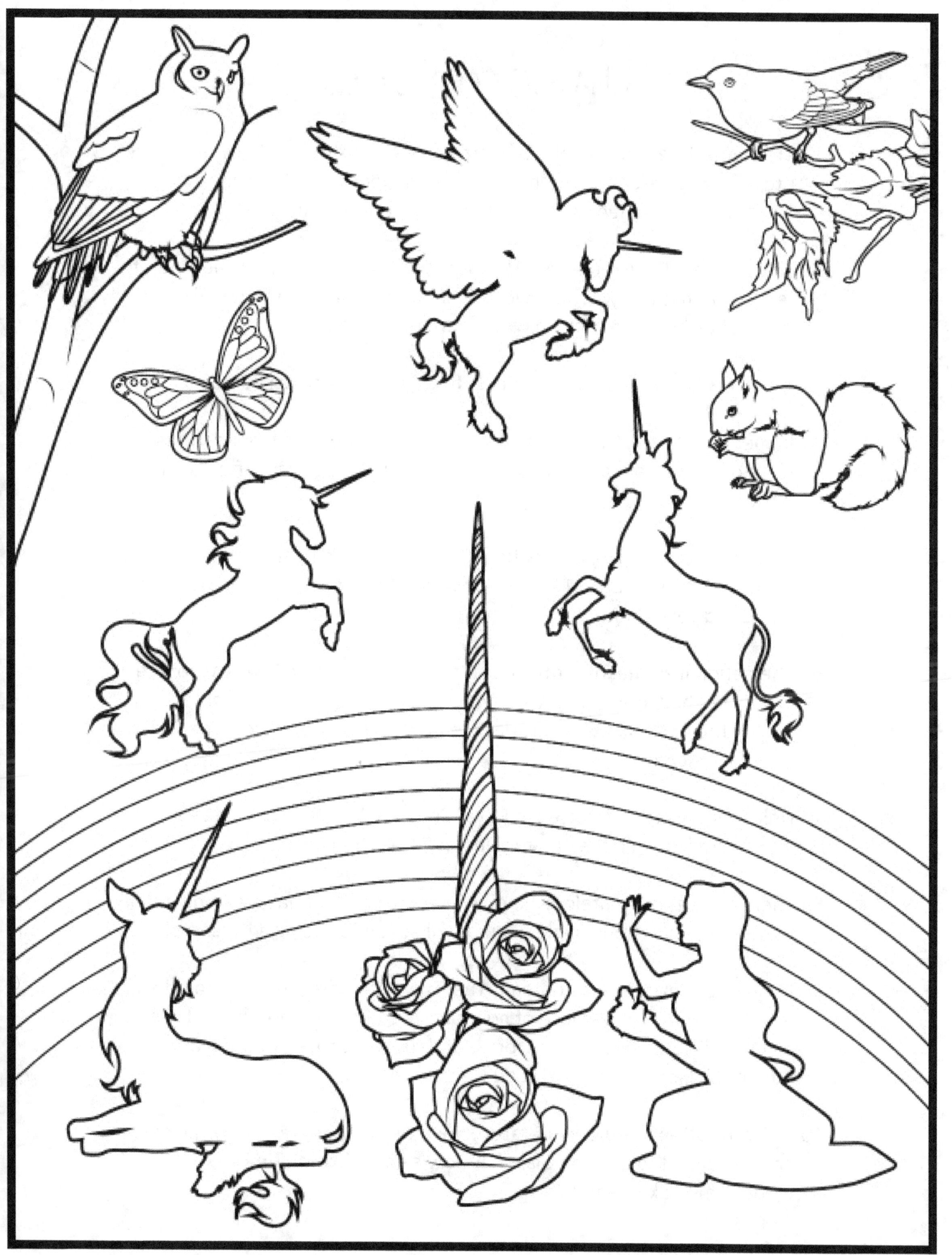

Unicorn Facts

1. The earliest description of a Unicorn came from the Greek historian, Ctesias, who described them as wild asses, fleet of foot, having a horn a cubit and a half in length, and coloured white, red, and black.

2. So sure were the Greeks that Unicorns actually existed, that they didn't feature in mythology. There were, instead, detailed in natural history texts. They believed that Unicorns were native to India.

3. A Unicorn's horn is said to be made from a substance called Alicorn

4. In medieval times, the tusks of Narwhals and other horned creatures were often sold as Unicorn horns for medicinal purposes- often to cure poisoning.

5. Unicorns, or Unicorn-like creatures, are mentioned in ancient texts from cultures around the world. The King James Bible mentions them six times in the Old Testament.

6. The national animal of Scotland is the Unicorn because it was seen as a proud and haughty beast, which would rather die than be captured. During the 15th and 16th centuries they even used a Gold Coin that was called a Unicorn.

7. Unicorns are often depicted in Royal Coats of Arms and can be seen, along with a lion, in the one for Queen Elizabeth II.

8. There's a breed of antelope, known as the Oryx, that has two long, thin horns and, from some angles, can be mistaken for being a Unicorn.

9. In America any start-up company that is worth more than a billion dollars is called a Unicorn (because of how rare it is). Those worth more than ten billion dollars are called Decacorns, and those worth more than one hundred billion dollars are called Hectocorns.

10. Unicorns often feature in literature. Two of the most well known works are "Through the Looking Glass" by Lewis Carroll, and "Timon of Athens" by William Shakespeare.

11. Harry Potter, Draco Malfoy and Fang found a Unicorn corpse when they were travelling through the Forbidden Forest.

12. The Qilin is a Unicorn-like creature that features in Chinese mythology. They are either fully or partially scaled, and shaped like an ox, deer, or a horse.

13. Marco Polo claimed to have seen Unicorns during his visits to the island Java in Indonesia. He said that they were scarcely smaller than an elephant, have the hair of a buffalo and feet of an elephant.

14. It's thought you can capture a Unicorn by standing in front of a tree. When it charges at you, if you move out of the way at the last moment its horn will become stuck. Remember, though, even if you do capture one, it is impossible to tame a Unicorn and they will always do whatever they want.

15. The word Unicorn traces back to the Latin word "Unicornis", which means "Single Horn".

16. During excavations at the sites of the ancient Indus Valley Civilisation, small stone seals were found with depictions of Unicorns on them. They are more than 4,500 years old.

17. Unicorns love rainbows. The phrase "Unicorns and Rainbows" refers to the feeling of perpetual bliss.

18. The Unicorn is thought to have the power to divine truth, and will pierce the heart of a liar with its horn.

19. Unicorn's eyes are usually blue or purple. Their hooves are normally golden.

20. The last known sighting of a Unicorn in the UK was in August of 2014 during the super moon. It was seen at the Moreton-in-Marsh agricultural show, reared up as lambs were taking part in a competition, and vanished into the woods.

Unicorn Word Search

Can you find all the hidden words?

W	G	S	O	S	A	M	R	Z	T	S	I	A	Q	X
I	D	W	V	P	T	N	F	X	J	E	W	J	H	Y
N	R	A	U	U	D	H	A	D	O	E	J	E	I	T
G	O	L	D	C	O	I	N	E	I	H	R	V	H	B
E	P	S	D	R	B	A	T	F	P	A	E	E	L	A
D	T	K	S	E	L	J	A	Z	L	G	V	X	X	V
T	B	E	L	T	L	Y	S	D	M	T	T	Q	E	A
N	L	B	O	T	C	L	I	N	R	O	C	I	N	U
D	D	C	K	U	V	C	A	J	O	G	J	J	S	V
I	S	Y	Q	B	H	R	H	R	X	N	D	A	B	D
N	U	W	F	Y	W	O	B	N	I	A	R	W	T	M
Y	V	R	D	H	F	M	R	O	V	P	U	Y	G	M
V	O	M	A	L	Y	K	Y	N	B	K	S	Z	E	Z
W	A	L	F	W	Y	A	I	Y	X	C	D	F	O	S
A	J	S	H	X	N	X	K	A	V	W	A	Y	I	A

Buttercup	Heraldic	Narwhal	Spiralled
Fantasia	Horn	Rainbow	Unicorn
Gold Coin	Horse	Scotland	Winged

Unicorn Quiz

Questions

1. Which Royal Prince was given a hairbrush made with hair from a Unicorns mane?
2. The throne chair of Denmark is supposedly made entirely from which part of a Unicorn?
3. Which Roman Leader saw a Unicorn in a German forest during his conquest of Gaul?
4. Marco Polo supposedly saw Unicorns on his travels, but which type of large, horned, animal is it thought he actually saw?
5. How does a Unicorn get its strength?
6. On what day, every year, do the Scots celebrate National Unicorn Day?
7. The Lascaux Caves are home to some of the earliest paintings that seem to depict Unicorns, and they are over 15,000 years old. Which country are they in?
8. Which notorious leader, and founder of the Mongol empire, changed his mind about invading India when he came face to face with a Unicorn?
9. Which Scandinavian seafaring people used to sell Narwhal horns and pretend they came from Unicorns?
10. The Horn of Windsor is one of the Crown Jewels of the British monarchy. Martin Frobisher, an explorer, gave it to which Queen as a gift?
11. Are Unicorns Herbivores, Carnivores, or Omnivores?
12. How many Unicorns are currently on show at London Zoo?
13. Why did churches used to add pieces of Unicorn horn to their holy water?
14. Pliny the younger was a Roman writer who talked about the existence of Unicorns. Which volcano did he witness erupting in 79AD?
15. Monoceros is another word for a Unicorn, but from which language does it come from?
16. The One-Horned Siberian Unicorn once roamed the wilds of Siberia, but how many years ago was this?
17. Unicorns are mainly white, but occasionally their tails or manes can be which colour?
18. The Unicorn cave, where a number of artefacts were found, is in which European country?
19. In which Harry Potter book did they find a Unicorn?
20. Which of the following powers do Unicorns not have: The ability to see the truth, cure illness, immortality, or invisibility?

Unicorn Crossword

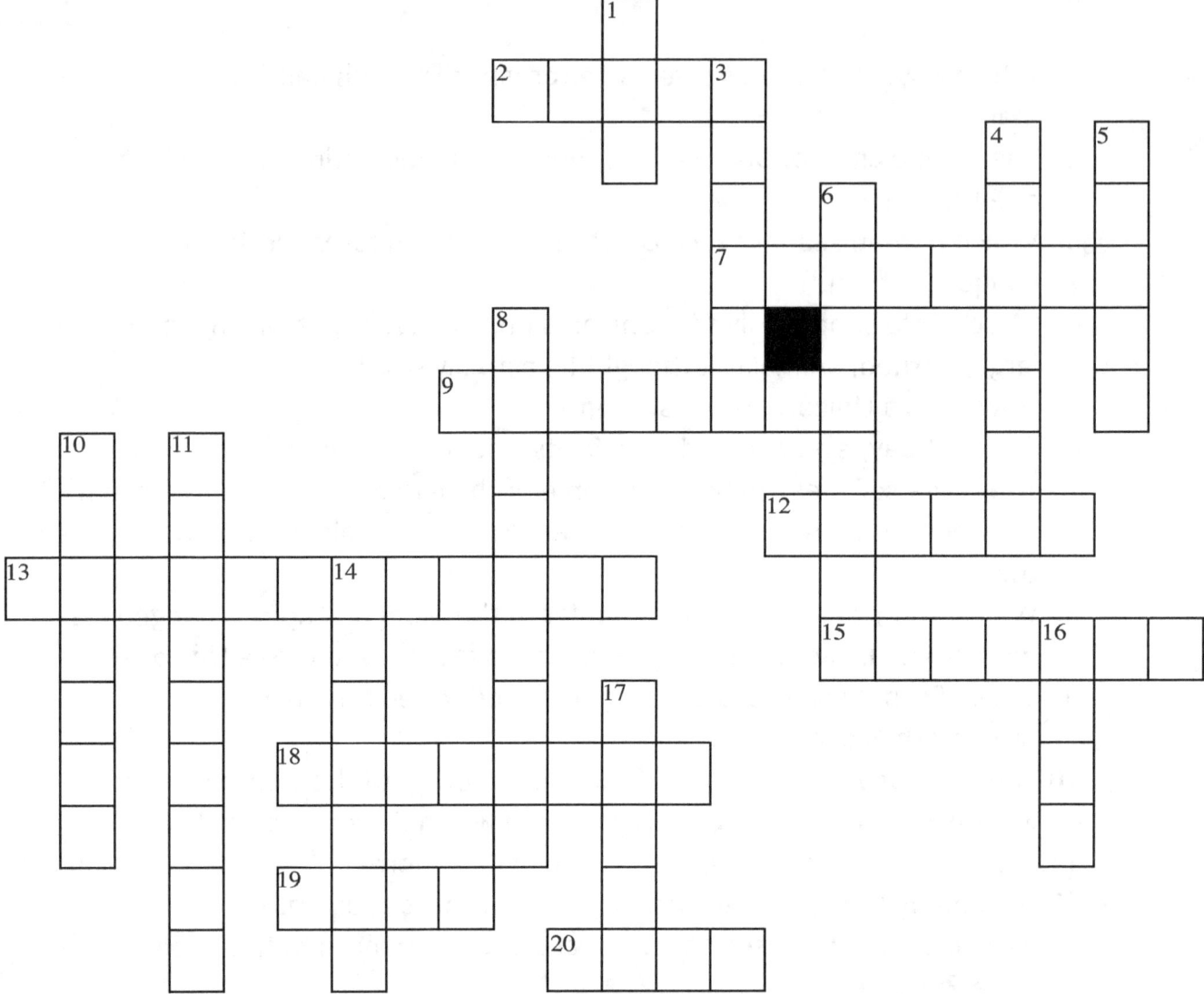

Across

2. The Qilin is a Unicorn-like creature that features in the mythology of which country? (5)

7. According to a Jewish legend, Unicorns are so strong they could even win in a fight against which giant long nosed creature? (8)

9. Which 1940 Disney film features Unicorns and a donkey wearing a Unicorn horn? (8)

12. What colour are a Unicorn's hooves? (6)

13. The author who featured the nursery rhyme characters of "The Lion and the Unicorn" in the book "Through the Looking Glass" (5, 7)

15. The marine creature that used to be hunted so its horn could be sold as that of a Unicorn (7)

18. The country whose national animal is the Unicorn (8)

19. The name of a type of antelope that has two long, thin horns that from some directions can look like a Unicorn (4)

20. Who was with Harry Potter and Draco Malfoy when they found the corpse of a Unicorn in the Forbidden Forest? (4)

Down

1. How many references to Unicorns are there in the Old Testament of the Bible? (3)

3. Timon of _____, the Shakespeare play that mentions a Unicorn (6)

4. Twilight _____, the unicorn from "My Little Pony" (7)

5. In "The Lion, The Witch, and the Wardrobe" movie, which of the Pevensie children rode a Unicorn? (5)

6. What do you get if you cross a Unicorn with a Pegasus? (8)

8. Famed explorer who saw Unicorns on his travels to Java (5, 4)

10. A Unicorn is the term used to describe a new company that is worth more than one billion dollars in which country? (7)

11. The first name of the European monarch who has a Unicorn and a lion on her coat of arms (9)

14. The Substance that a Unicorn's horn is made from (7)

16. Which part of the Unicorn was sold to cure poisoning? (4)

17. The country where the Greeks believed Unicorns to live (5)

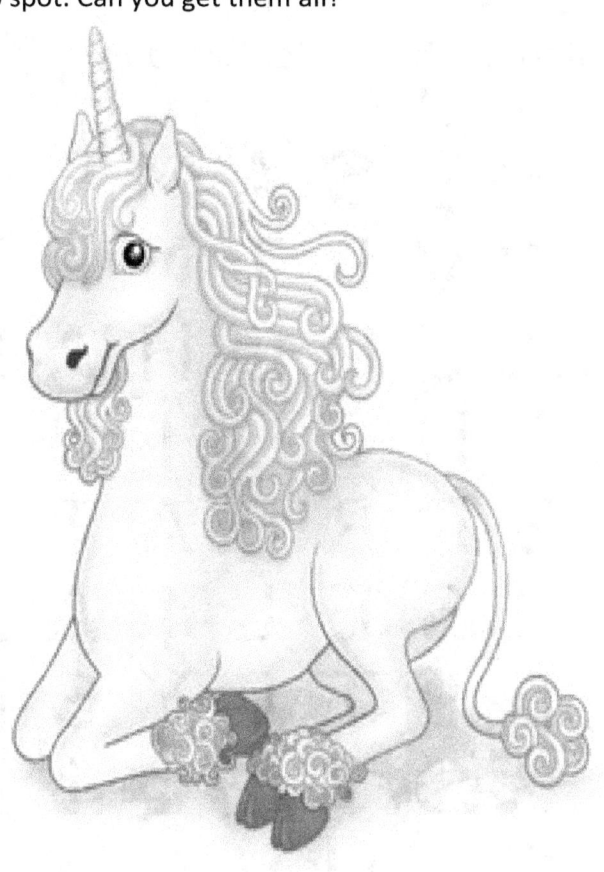

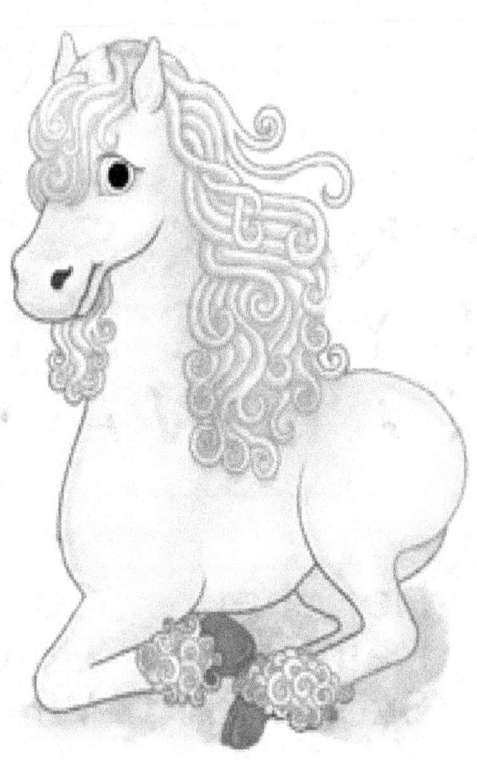

Unicorn Word Search

Can you find all the hidden words?

```
W G S O S A M R Z T S I A Q X
I D W V P T N F X J E W J H Y
N R A U U D H A D O E J E I T
G O L D C O I N E I H R V H B
E P S D R B A T F P A E E L A
D T K S E L J A Z L G V X X V
T B E L T L Y S D M T T Q E A
N L B O T C L I N R O C I N U
D D C K U V C A J O G J J S V
I S Y Q B H R H R X N D A B D
N U W F Y W O B N I A R W T M
Y V R D H F M R O V P U Y G M
V O M A L Y K Y N B K S Z E Z
W A L F W Y A I Y X C D F O S
A J S H X N X K A V W A Y I A
```

Buttercup	Heraldic	Narwhal	Spiralled
Fantasia	Horn	Rainbow	Unicorn
Gold Coin	Horse	Scotland	Winged

Answers

1. Prince George (although it's apparently used by the Duchess of Cambridge)
2. The Horn
3. Julius Caesar
4. A Rhinoceros
5. By absorbing sunrays
6. 9th of April
7. France
8. Genghis Khan
9. The Vikings
10. Queen Elizabeth I
11. Herbivores (The love to eat exotic and colourful flowers)
12. None (But sometimes they like to visit the other animals)
13. To purify it
14. Mount Vesuvius
15. Greek
16. At least 29,000 years ago
17. Rainbow
18. Germany (There's also another in Austria)
19. Harry Potter and the Philosopher's Stone
20. Invisibility

Spot The Difference

1. The Horn
2. The Right Leg
3. The Rear Left Hoof
4. The Tail
5. The White of its Eye
6. A Tuft of Hair From its Mane

Other Coloring Books from Aryla Publishing

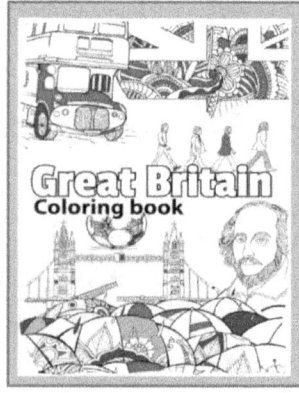

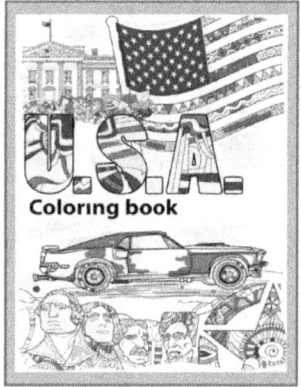

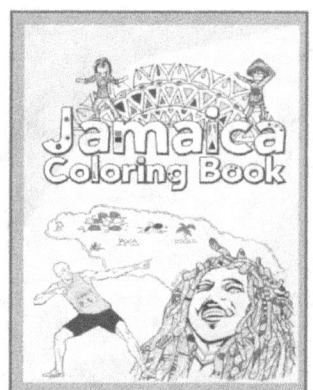

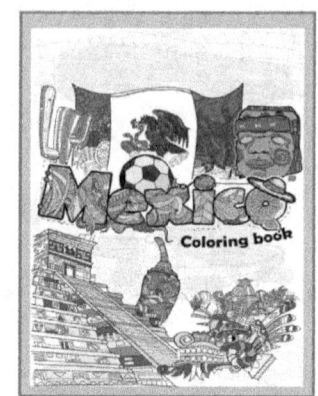

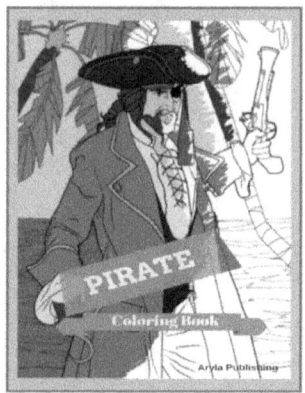

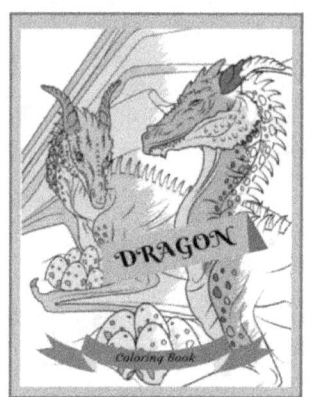

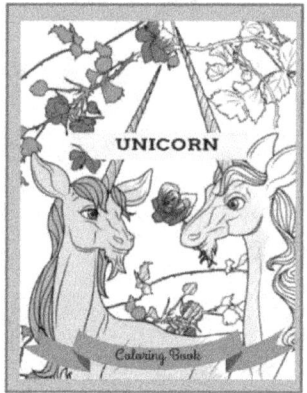

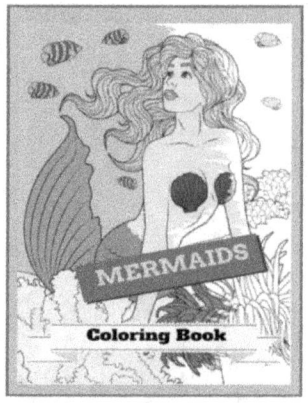

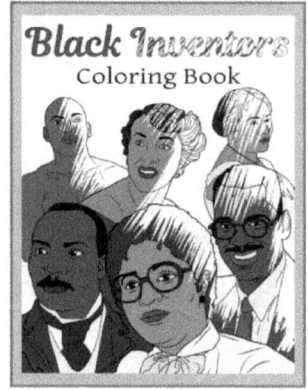

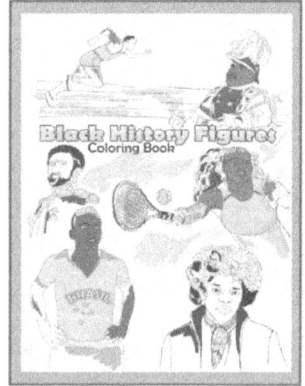

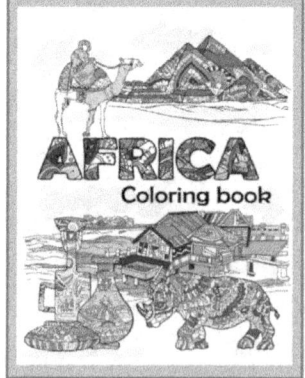

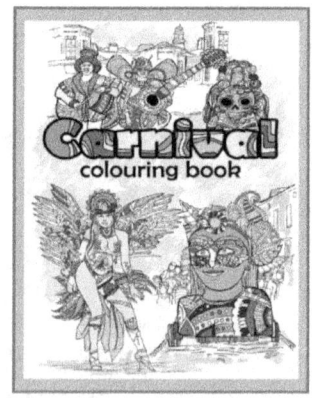

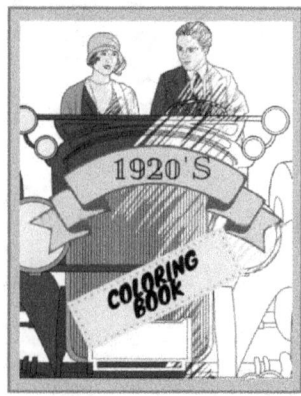

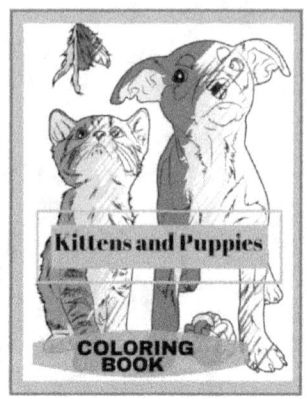

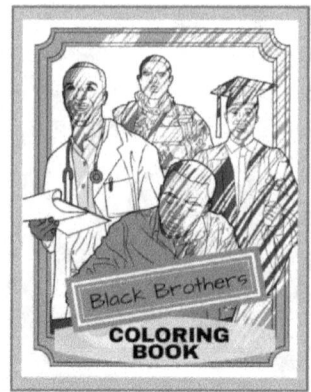

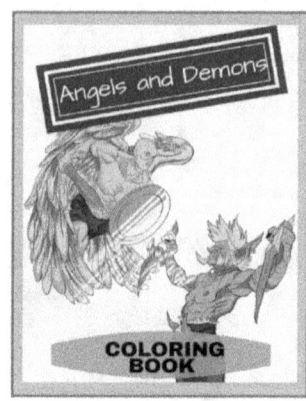

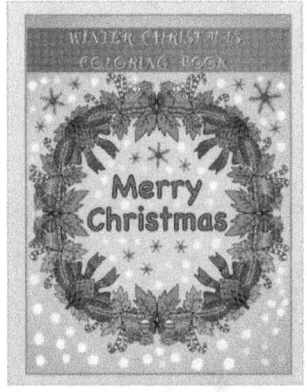
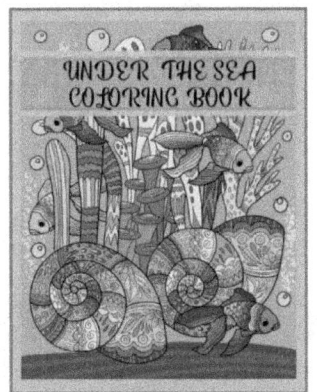
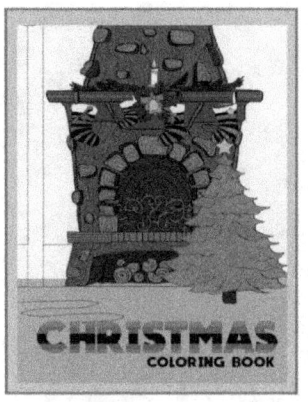
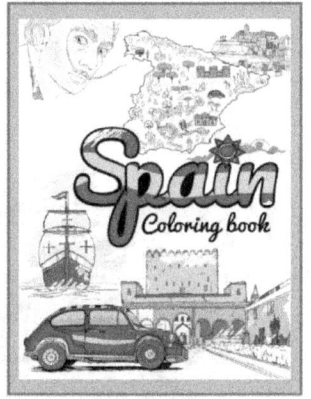
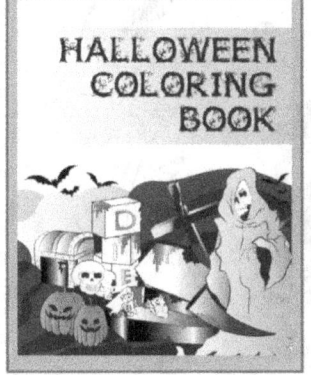
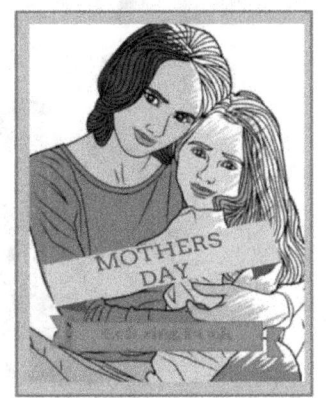
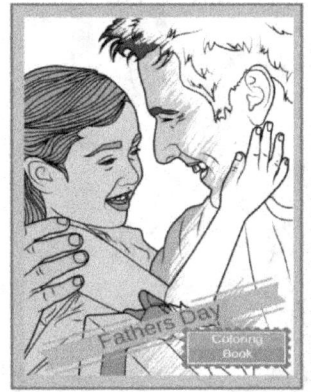
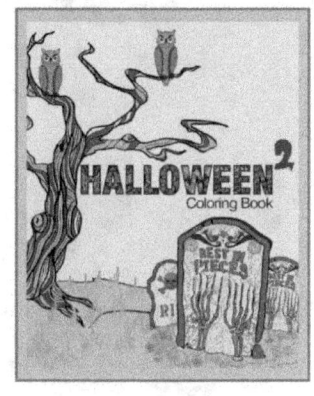
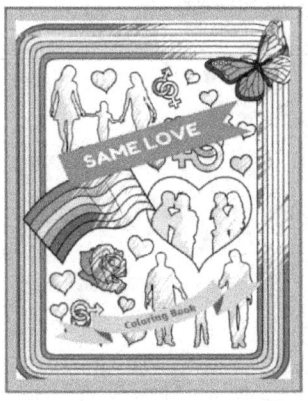
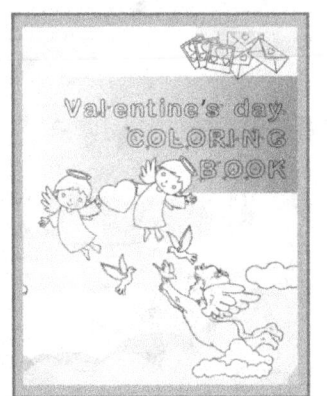
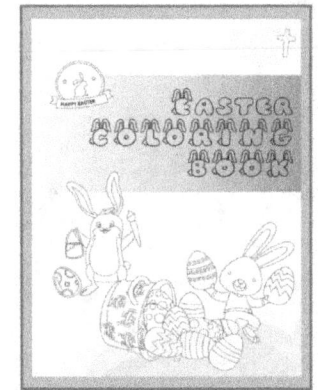
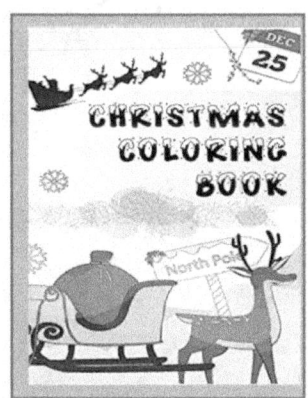

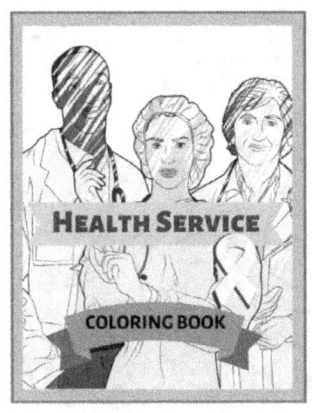
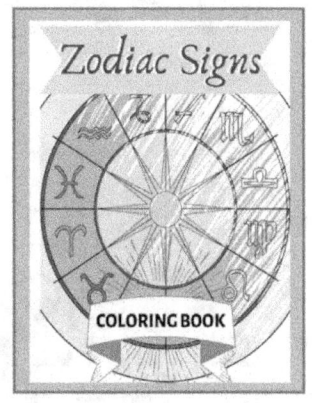
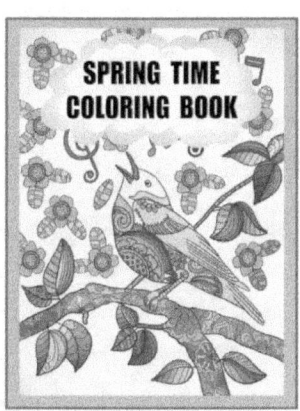

Color In Fun
Kids Books

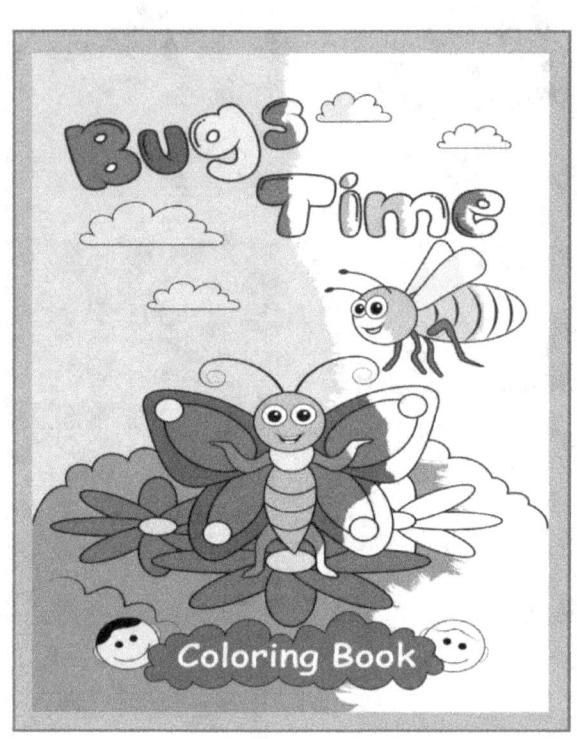

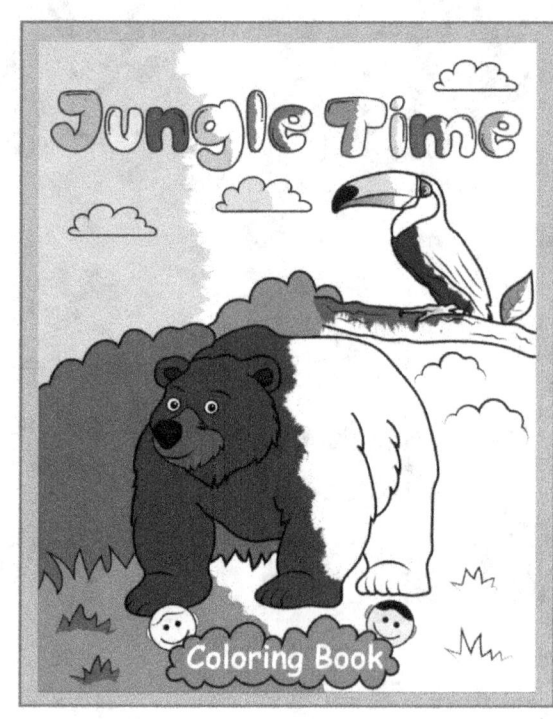

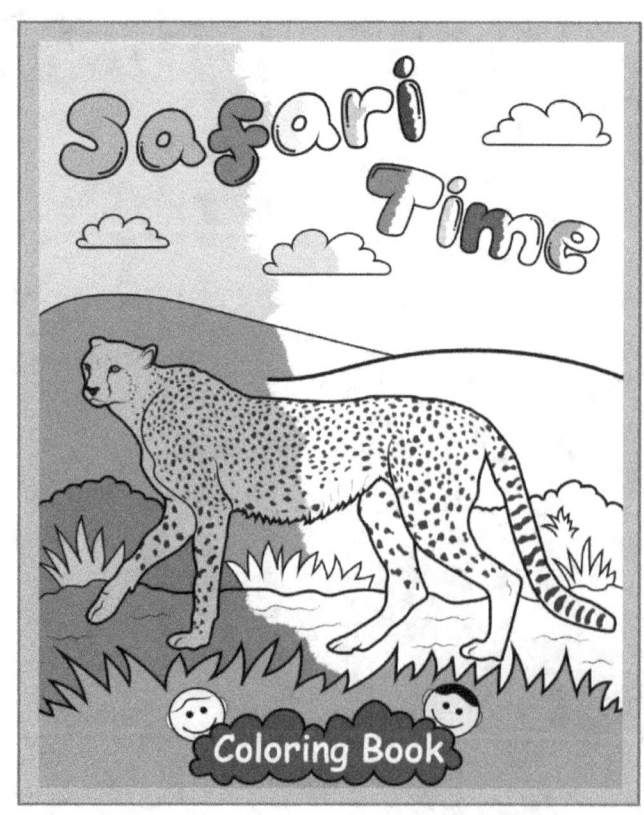

Thank you for purchasing this book.

If you would like to know more about Aryla Publishing Books please visit:-

www.ArylaPublishing.com

Or follow us on
Facebook
Twitter
Instagram
for *free promotions*

@arylapublishing

We would love to know what you think of this book so please leave us a review.

Have a wonderful day ☺

Visit **www.ArylaPublishing.com**
to find out about all new releases.

Follow us @arylapublishing on Twitter Instagram & Facebook

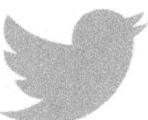  

Search for Aryla Publishing on

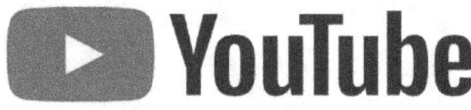 **YouTube**

Check out our <u>Book Trailers</u>

<u>Subscribe</u> to keep up to date with new releases!

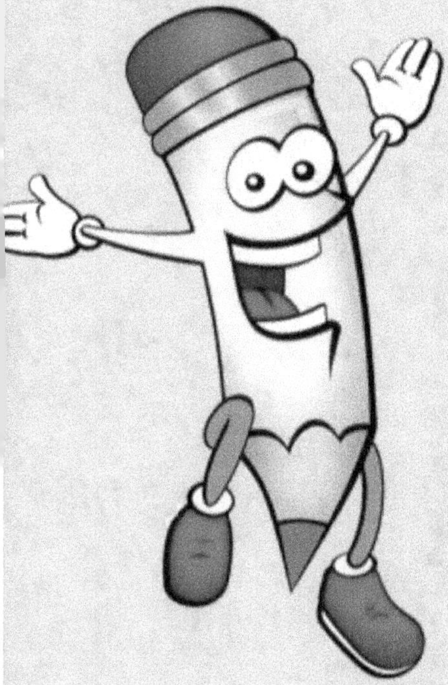

WE WOULD LOVE YOUR FEEDBACK

PLEASE LEAVE REVIEW AT:-

https://viewbook.at/unicorncolorreview

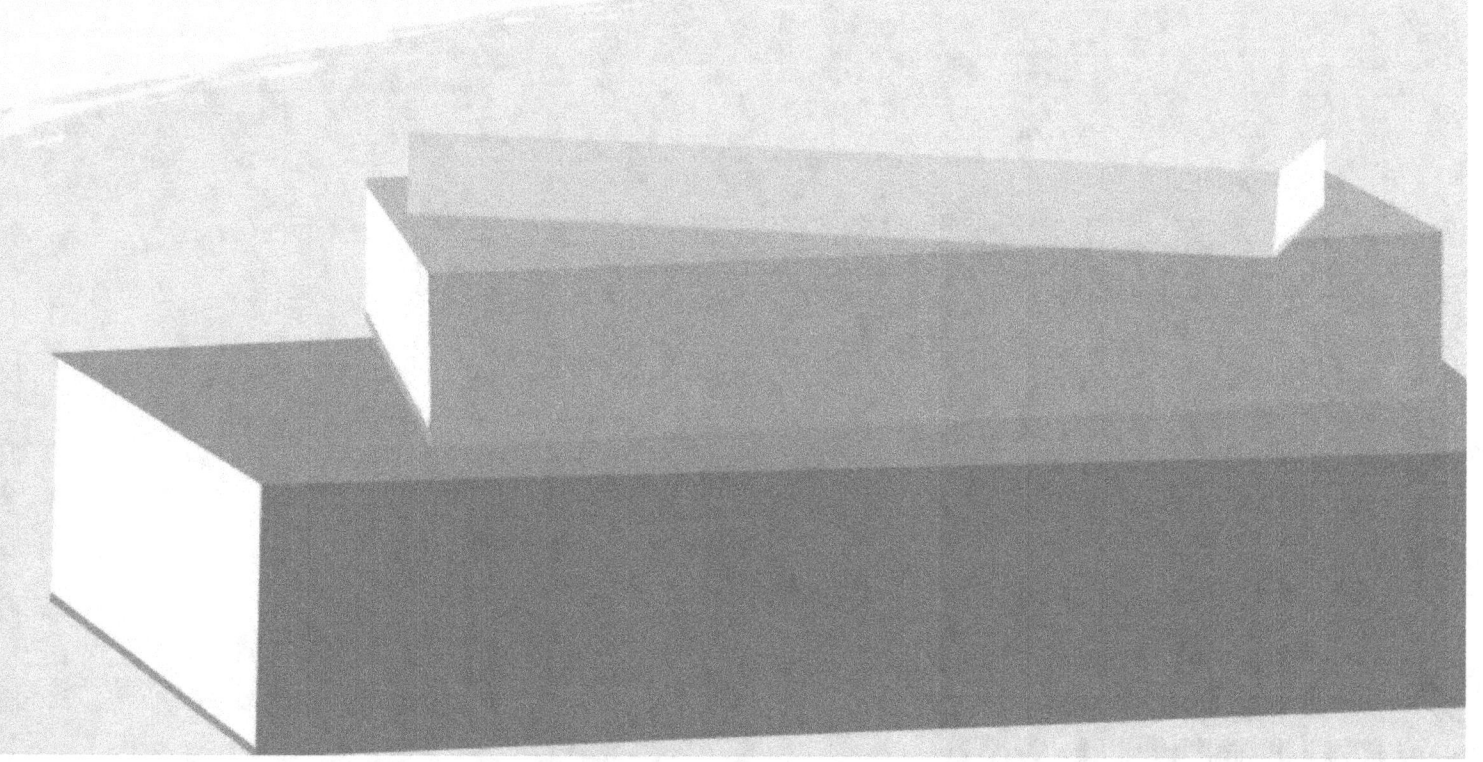